You Can Be Happy NOW

Merlin R. Carothers

Everyone desires to be happy!
This book will help you understand
how much GOD wants you to be happy.

ADDITIONAL TITLES BY
MERLIN R. CAROTHERS

Prison to Praise
Power in Praise
Answers to Praise
Praise Works!
Walking and Leaping
Bringing Heaven Into Hell
Victory on Praise Mountain
More Power to You
What's on Your Mind?
Let Me Entertain You
From Fear to Faith
Prison to Praise (Video movie)

Cover photo by Edee Pawlik

Published in Escondido, CA
www.merlincarothers.com
Copyright © 2001 by Merlin R. Carothers
ISBN 0-943026-34-2
Printed in the United States of America

Unless otherwise noted, Scriptures taken from the Holy Bible: New International Version®, NIV®, copyright © 1973, 1978, 1984, by International Bible Society. Used by permission of Zondervan Publishing House. The "NIV" and "New International Version" trademarks are registered in the United States Patent and Trademark Office by International Bible Society.

Scripture quotations from the Holy Bible noted: KJV are from the King James Version of the Bible.

NKJ are from The New King James Version, copyright © 1979, 1980, 1982, Thomas Nelson, Inc. Publishers (used by permission).

TLB are taken from The Living Bible, copyright 1971 by Tyndale House Publisher, Wheaton, IL (used by permission).

AMP are from The Amplified Bible: Old Testament. Copyright © 1962, 1964 by Zondervan Publishing House (used by permission); and from The Amplified New Testament. Copyright © 1958 by the Lockman Foundation (used by permission).

MSG are taken from The Message, Copyright © by Eugene Peterson, 1993, 1994, 1995 (used by permission of Nav Press Publishing Group).

NCV quoted from New Century Version, copyright © 1987, 1988, 1991 by Word Publishing, Nashville, TN (used by permission).

Dedication

My special appreciation to my dear wife, Mary, who has edited, advised and supported me in this book, and in everything I do. Her skill and spiritual wisdom have caused my work to be far better than I could have ever done alone.

Prologue

Writing this book has been extraordinarily exciting to me. I have often felt compelled to stop other work in order to add new revelations. I've been awakened during the night with surprising insights to questions people have asked.

Each additional inspiration made me feel as if I was participating in something unique. I pray that as you read this book, these insights will be a blessing to you and bring you happiness.

Contents

Bubbling With Happiness

Happiness: So universally sought, but seemingly elusive. Since Adam and Eve rebelled against God and were cast from the Garden of Eden, mankind has sought the happiness only God can give. But many people exist on a meager portion of happiness. If you are one of those folks, I have wonderful news: you can have and enjoy the happiness that comes to everyone who sincerely seeks it.

Consider the unsightly weeds. They spring up everywhere and need no encouragement. But flowers must be planted, fertilized, watered and given regular care. Unhappiness springs up easily and needs no special assistance, but acquiring happiness requires patient effort.

I have been blessed to know people who bubbled with happiness. What a witness they were to me! They inspired me to want to learn their secret for joy, since for many years I thought I could never get over my natural tendency to feel sorry for myself at every opportunity – a self-pity that made me quick to snap at anyone who disrupted the peace and tranquility that I craved.

Our human nature wants everything to be exactly as we desire before we can be happy. This is why we need the help of the Holy Spirit to have His joy. Many of us find it difficult to believe that God *can* increase our happiness, but as you read this book you will discover how He does just that! Get ready for an exciting trip! Your life will never be the same again.

A Joy to Learn

With God's gentle but persistent prodding, I began to realize that I grumbled about something at least a hundred times a day. When the spirit of grumbling ensnares us, we don't realize that it has become so much a part of our lives. I certainly didn't!

I started off each day grumbling the moment I was jarred awake by the loud clanging of my alarm clock. I grumbled even before my eyes opened: "I wish I didn't have to get up so early, I muttered. Why do I have to get up so early all the time? It's not even five a.m.!"

Then, stumbling to the bathroom, I grumbled at the growing number of aches and pains. At the mirror I saw how terrible I looked, then chided myself for wasting time on such foolishness. I needed to hurry or I would be late. The weather, too, caused me to grumble. It was always too cold or too hot.

Everything was too this or too that. I didn't verbalize all my complaints, of course, but grumbled away in my thoughts and in my heart. I was firmly and painfully ensnared in Satan's "grumbling trap." And I was displeasing God.

God persistently guided me to scriptures such as, *Rejoice in the Lord always* (Ph. 4:4), but I was slow to heed and learn. I certainly was not a living example of an *always rejoicing* Christian. It was easy to excuse myself though – everyone I knew grumbled. Most did so aloud.

Fortunately, God didn't permit me to get away with such excuses. More and more I saw that I did not measure up to God's standard for His people. But how to change?

Step-by-step He persuaded me to try, and I could

not resist His loving insistence.

Perhaps this book is God's loving insistence to *you*. Maybe you, too, have become an accomplished grumbler without even realizing it. Start listening to your thoughts. How frequently do you express the attitude, "I am not happy, so I am not rejoicing"?

Seeing ourselves as grumblers is painful. But out of the pain comes hope. As we learn how to receive new instruction from God, we realize that He is helping us become the happy person that *He* wants us to be.

Soon we see a smile on our face when we look in the mirror. We can actually *feel* a desire to tell God how happy we are over the new joy He is helping us to find.

Praise to God that comes from the heart puts a light in our eyes, a spring in our steps – and a blessed knowledge that God is actually working in us.

What *joy*! What *gladness* to know that God is using each moment, whether pleasant or painful, to prepare us for our eternal dwelling place – Heaven. There will be no grumbling there! We must get ready. We can! And it is a joy to learn how.

A Little Child Shall Lead Them

One day while serving in Vietnam, I suddenly realized that I wanted to laugh, sing and skip. I felt like I was walking a foot above the ground. Earlier that day, though, every part of me had ached and I had felt anything *but* wonderful. When I went to our doctor, he said I had a fever and gave me pills to take. Those pills made me forget every ache I had, and for a few hours I actually *enjoyed* being in Vietnam! But was I *really* happy? No! My elation was merely a fleeting, pill-induced euphoria. Everyone wants to know how to obtain – and keep – real, lasting happiness.

False joy comes in all kinds of attractive-looking

3

packages. A pill can make us feel as if every part of our body is happy. A few drinks of alcohol can make sorrows and sadness *seem* to fade away. We have no problem *finding* "joy", but temporary jolts of joy are just that – temporary. Then, disappointed, we might complain to God and ask Him why He designed us to seek joy, yet made us so that nothing seems to give us *lasting* happiness. His answer? He wants us to find *His* solution – the *real* source of happiness.

One Easter Sunday I met a young father and mother and their nearly three-year-old daughter. I had never seen the little girl before, but she acted as if I was her special friend. She hugged my legs and said "Happy Easter," then began to laugh as she jumped up and down. Her joy was a sight to behold. Her amused mother said, "She wasn't like this until last Easter, when her personality completely changed." Then the parents told me a remarkable story.

One year earlier the mother and the father, who was Jewish, had become Christians and were baptized in the ocean. During the ceremony the then two-year-old daughter waded out into the edge of the water to watch. When the parents came up out of the water, she did something quite unusual. The little girl began to jump up and down in the water, and laughed with such joy that everyone could see that something had happened to her. She reached down, picked up sand from the bottom and threw it into the air as if she was celebrating something. The mother said, "She's been like this ever since that day a year ago. God did something remarkable in her."

When I asked the mother why she thought God had done this, she told me how God was using her little daughter in a completely unexpected way. Whenever her husband's Jewish parents come to see them, their granddaughter carries a Bible to them and says things such as, "I love the Bible" or, "Let's pray with the Bible." Then she shows such happy excitement as she tells them how much she loves Jesus, that they are never offended. They often come just to see her.

As I watched the little girl, I thought of what a good object lesson she is to us. Joy that comes from God has a quality about it that brings laughter into the soul, and equips us to effectively tell others about Jesus.

Bless the Judge

At the heart of spiritual joy is the secret of finding happiness in the midst of things that other people find unpleasant.

For thousands of years alchemists sought a formula to turn inferior metals into gold. That equation evaded them, but God has provided His children with an infinitely greater treasure – His formula to turn sadness and despair into joy – His joy.

Just as God placed enormous power within a single tiny atom, He also concealed joy in unexpected places. It is our challenge to discover His "treasures of joy." And with God's help we can. We can find fulfillment and joy in things that other people find unpleasant. Such is the heart of spiritual joy.

The Amplified Bible provides an interesting translation of Luke 7:23: *To be envied is he who . . . is not hurt or resentful or annoyed or repelled or made to stumble whatever may occur*. People, places and circumstances that can tie us into knots, surround us. But each of these holds within them the seeds of potential joy.

Quite often I receive letters from anxious people who relate their severe problems and who stress their inability to find anything good in their circumstances. They are definitely not joyful. Yet I receive letters

5

from others pressed by similar circumstances who express joy in their situations. Why the difference in attitude? The latter had learned God's secret of finding joy in their problems, whereas the former had not. Negative people and circumstances surround us daily but, if we persevere, we too can learn to find joy – whatever our circumstances. A letter I received from a young jail inmate provides an encouraging case in point.

This eighteen-year-old had been arrested for burglary and possession of drugs. In jail he was given a copy of *Prison to Praise*. He read it twice and carried it with him when scheduled to go before the judge. In court, his appointed attorney told him the parole officer had recommended that he receive a thirty-year sentence. The young man clutched his book and prayed, "God, whatever You want, I accept. I will serve You wherever I go."

The judge said, "These are serious charges," and then studied the young man intently. "What is that you are carrying?" When the youth held up his copy of *Prison to Praise,* the judge said, "May I have a look at it?" Leafing through it, the judge recessed the court and went to his chambers. Two hours later he returned and opened the court. "Young man, do you believe what is in this book?"

"Yes sir, I do," was the reply.

"Very well, I'm going to sentence you to only five years, less the time you have been confined. And may I keep this book?"

The young man floated out of court, went back to his cell and knelt to pray. He writes, "Now wherever I go, I know that Jesus will be with me. I found Him here. I am praying that God will use *Prison to Praise* to bless the judge." The same jail that brings bitterness and despondency to one man is now bringing life and joy to another.

I receive many, many letters from people around the world who joyfully relate how God has shared His secret of finding happiness in all their circumstances. God works in amazing ways His wonders to perform. He invites you to discover His treasures in whatever experiences you are having.

Our Main Reason to be Happy

Why would I encourage you to have a heart that is overflowing with happiness? Some reasons would be valid, but not paramount.

Having joy causes us to enjoy life, but pleasing ourselves is not the main objective for followers of Jesus.

Having joy improves our health, but Jesus did not teach us to make decisions based primarily on what would keep us healthy.

Having joy pleases those who have to live or work with us. But we know that Jesus did not spend His life trying to please people. His emphasis was always on one thing – pleasing God. And there we have our *main* reason for having hearts that are filled with joy – pleasing God.

Romans 14:17 tell us: *For, after all, the important thing for us as Christians is . . . stirring up goodness and peace and joy from the Holy Spirit.* Every day holds many opportunities for us to discover secrets of receiving – joy from the Holy Spirit.

Jesus wants us to have joy, and He was willing to pay a terrible price to make that possible. In John 15:11 (TLB), Jesus told His disciples one of the goals He had for those who would follow Him: *I have told you this so that you will be filled with my joy.*

We all have times when we prefer to be grumpy

or out-of-sorts with the world. But followers of Christ are called to please God, rather than themselves. This confirms that our main reason to be happy is to please our Heavenly Father and, in so doing, be happier than we have ever been!

Everything Perfect

We aren't too inclined to live perfect lives ourselves, but we are fully persuaded that everything should be perfect *for us*.

Since childhood we have chafed under any situation that wasn't quite to our liking. We wanted to look great, be smart, have the most popular friends, etc. But by now we have learned that life seldom measures up to our standard of perfection. We have learned to adapt to this state of affairs, although sometimes not too gracefully. Nevertheless, we still cling to our old passion — "Oh that everything would be perfect for me."

Past disappointments may have severely dampened our expectations. Our hopes and dreams may have been shattered, and sometimes we may even have felt that God had let us down. We haven't always understood how to take advantage of His offer in Philippians 4:19 (TLB) which says, *He who will supply all your needs . . . because of what Christ Jesus has done for us.*

Our intellect may think, *God has never supplied all of my needs and He probably never will.* But the reason for our confusion may be our misunderstanding of how God sees time differently from us. He sees tomorrow as clearly as if it were yesterday! He knows *The end from the beginning* (Is. 46:10).

We want God to change our situation *now*, so we can have what we want *now*. But God may have a

8

better plan. He may want to change *us*.

For much of my life I had a big problem with Philippians 4:19, because God rarely seemed to supply my needs. When I had what I considered a "need," I would tell God that I believed He would supply that need. Sometimes I would close my eyes while I prayed, and tell Him I believed that when I opened my eyes, there in front of me would be the thing I "needed." If that didn't produce the result I wanted (and of course it didn't), I would try again and again, until discouraged, I finally gave up. My faith just wasn't strong enough, I thought. This severely strained my relationship with God.

Let me use an illustration to explain. If I thought I needed a car, my flesh was quite sure that I really did *need* it, and the sooner the better. If God was my provider, then He *needed* to supply the car as soon as possible. At that time my main focus centered on what I believed God *should do,* since He had promised to supply whatever I needed. Then I learned a principle that strengthened my faith, and made my communion with God something that gives me ever-increasing joy.

The important principle I learned was that God had *already* supplied my *need* for a car. I came to understand that *every* "need" I had was a clear fulfillment of Philippians 4:19! From that point on, my peace of mind improved wonderfully. My so-called needs sometimes gave me more joy than if God had supplied the material things. Remember how the Israelites struggled in the wilderness because they "needed" water and better tasting food? God wanted to lead them into The Promised Land, but He did not because they failed to believe that the shortages they had were exactly what they *needed*!

God *does* supply His children whatever they need. That is the foundation of our faith! We should rejoice in whatever God is supplying *now.* By rejoicing in God's goodness our faith and happiness will continue to increase.

The Power of One Smile

Jesus said, Let your light so shine before men, that they may see your good works, and glorify your Father in heaven (Mt. 5:16 NKJV).

In verse 14 Jesus said, *You are the light of the world.* As the Holy Spirit continued to open my heart to new insights, I realized that Jesus was emphasizing the light that is *in* us. Light that is in us should shine so that *others* can see it! If we have real joy in our hearts, people *will* see it in our faces and even in our eyes.

You have probably heard the expression, "His face lit up with a smile." Smiles often reveal an inner joy. A heart-felt smile can open the doors to other people's hearts and, in turn, bless the one who smiles. Remember: *Give, and it will be given unto you.*

While still in the Army I attended a large gathering of Christian businessmen. The man in charge saw me enter the auditorium, and said "Colonel Carothers, come up to the platform and tell everyone why you are so happy."

As I spoke to the thousands of men assembled there, my joy caused many doors to open through which I could share the message of praise. I began to carry a suitcase full of *Prison to Praise* books to each meeting. Eventually those meetings launched the distribution of millions of Praise Books. In time, that one smile of joy opened doors for me to speak in forty-nine states. God had used one smile to accomplish His purpose. Since then I've seen Him use the power of joy to accomplish many other good things.

The brighter God's light in us becomes, the more people will see it and thereby find their way to Him. It is not selfish of us to want more of God's joy, for the more of it we have, the clearer we show the way for others.

One of my greatest delights is to have strangers say to me, "You seem so happy." That opens the door for me to ask, "Would you like to know *why* I am so happy?"

On another occasion I attended a Christian program held in a large stadium. Along with 40,000 others I was hurrying to show my ticket, get through the gate and find a good seat. But when I gave my ticket to the agent, he surprised me by holding out his hand for me to stop. I thought, *something is wrong with my ticket.* The agent said, "I've been watching people come through here for an hour, and you are the first one with a big smile on his face. Thank you." I wasn't aware that I had been smiling, but apparently my inner joy had been shining through. The man went on to say, "Your smile makes me feel good." I thanked him in turn, then urged him to attend the meeting.

The joy that God gives us, His children, will ultimately manifest itself in our outward appearance. Our joyful appearance, in turn, may inspire those who see us to accept Jesus as their Savior.

Let your light shine. If it needs to be brighter, praise God that He is increasing its intensity. Practice thanking Him for His joy. We will never get into trouble with God for wanting more of His light to shine in us. He has already told us that the light shining in us will cause *men to glorify Him.* And when we glorify Him, His Spirit creates ever-greater joy in us!

Faith That Works – NOW

This wonderful news – the message that God wants to save us – has been given to us just as it was to those who lived in the time of Moses. But it didn't do them any good because they didn't believe it. They didn't mix it with faith (He. 4:2 TLB).

I had meditated on this verse many times over the years, but much of its meaning had escaped me. Then the Holy Spirit revealed a new and vital insight: if we are to receive God's salvation we must have *faith* – we must *believe*! And we must *believe* in order to enjoy His happiness! Paul affirms this in verse three: *Only we who believe God can enter into his place of rest.*

For 400 years the Jews had awaited the time when they could enter into the Promised Land (His rest). They desperately wanted to enter, but they didn't *believe* – and because of their unbelief they did not receive God's blessing. In verse nine Paul says: *There is a full complete rest still waiting for the people of God.*

This passage intrigued me, so I canceled many activities in order to have more time to hear the Holy Spirit speak to me. As I listened I began to realize that we Christians often miss the full and complete rest that even now awaits us. I increased my efforts to follow Paul's instructions: *Let us do our best to go into that place of rest, too, being careful not to disobey God as the children of Israel did, thus failing to get in* (Vs. 11).

My attention focused especially on learning not to disobey God as the children of Israel did. Their disobedience was centered in one thing: They would not believe. There have been times when I failed to believe as well. Even after I learned to believe that God would eventually work things out for my good, I had remained unhappy while I waited for Him to do so. That had seemed logical to me then, but now I was seeing that it was not logical to God! If I was going to be what He wanted me to be, I needed to learn how to center my attention on believing Him now, not at some time in the future.

Many Bible verses urge us to receive God's joy. God wants us to believe that His joy is powerful, and able to overcome even our worst problems. Certainly we want to obey verse eleven: *Being careful not to disobey God as the children of Israel did . . . for the clear warning is . . . thus failing to get in.*

Believing says, "I am now filled with His joy." *Doubting says,* "Oh God, please give me peace and joy. I need it."

Believing means to *Rejoice in the Lord always. Again I will say, rejoice!* (Ph. 4:4 NKJV).

Rejoicing is obedience. Obedience, in turn, causes us to realize – to *know* that, *Whatever God says to us is full of living power* (He. 4:12 TLB). Our part is to believe His Word! We don't even have to understand – only believe it.

The necessity of belief was becoming increasingly clear to me. The seed of faith was growing within me, and soon I was learning to enjoy the abundant harvest of believing Him.

When I expect joy to bless me only at some future time, it remains elusive. But when I believe that it is mine now – it *becomes mine now*!

In God's Presence

The God of hope fill you with all joy and peace in believing . . . (Ro. 15:13 KJV).

For years I had tried to greet people in a joyful manner. When they said "Hello," I tried to respond with an enthusiasm that exceeded theirs. But then something began to happen. I started to respond to greetings with a new zeal. My words became stronger, more forceful. The more joy I conveyed to the others, the more positive were their responses to me. They paid closer attention. They smiled, perked up and received new joy in themselves. The Holy Spirit was working *His joy* in them! Seeing this gave me even more incentive to let Him speak through me. I was especially inspired when I saw sad faces light up. It was as if, somehow, they knew I was a Christian without my saying even a word about my faith. The joy in me was reaching out to their spirits, touching them in the deepest part of their hearts.

It became clearer to me that *the fruit of the Spirit is...joy and peace* (see Gal. 5:22). And the more I felt His presence in my heart, the more I realized how far I was from the goals He has given us.

I had understood that *in God's presence there is fulness of joy* (Ps. 16:11 KJV), and that we would have that fullness of joy when someday we enter into His presence in Heaven. But, now, something new began to dawn on me.

God, Himself, is surrounded by joy! Wherever He is, there is joy.

So when we enter into His joy, we are entering His presence!

The less joy we have, the farther we are from His presence!

When we are surrounded by, and abide in, His joy - we are in His presence!

The power of God's Spirit reaches out to defeat the suffering that Satan has inflicted upon our world. The Old Testament frequently urged God's people to be joyful. Deuteronomy 12:7 told them they were to: *Rejoice in everything you have put your hand to, because the LORD your God has blessed you.*

The Promised Land was a *type* of the new Kingdom of God that Jesus came to introduce. In Jesus' Kingdom we should *rejoice in all that we do*.

In Deuteronomy 16:12 (TLB) God told the Jews: *Remember! You were a slave in Egypt, so be sure to carry out this command*. We must remember that we, too, were once slaves – to sin; but because of Christ we now have much more reason to rejoice than the Old Testament Israelites ever did!

Good Medicine

Here is an interesting item that caught my attention. A study compiled and released by a Dr. Michael Murray suggests that amazing things happen when people smile.

According to Murray, smiling causes changes in the flow of blood to certain areas of the brain, changes that release endorphins and other important mood-elevating compounds. Smiling, he says, can act as a powerful anti-depressant that can trigger numerous other health benefits as well.

Anti-depressant drugs can cause harmful side effects, but smiling can have only good effects on the body. I always knew that when we feel good we are more likely to smile. Now I realize that the reverse is also true – when we smile we are also more likely to feel better!

Psalm 139:14 says, *I will praise you because I am fearfully and wonderfully made.* The more I learn about the way God designed our bodies, the more I understand that He built His laws within us. When we obey Him by rejoicing, we feel better and enjoy better health.

Our bodies have remarkable self-healing powers that can defeat almost any germ that might invade them. I've seen people live for months in unsanitary conditions that could easily have caused illness, yet they remained well. Deadly germs exist all around us, but our resilient bodies are usually able to resist them.

Unfortunately, however, our bodies are often unable to resist the "germ of unhappiness". This nasty germ can work its way through our minds and emotions, ultimately affecting our bodies. The Good News, though, is that Jesus came to the world to defeat unhappiness. He came to offer us joy and peace of mind (see Is. 53:5). If we want more peace and joy, we can learn to receive it. How? By rejoicing in our confidence that God is working His good *in* us and *for* us, and by *accepting* the joy His Son came to give us. When we do these things we release God's power to work good for us.

If we learn to receive more joy, our spirits will cause the joy to work good things in us whether we are awake or asleep! This is the way our wise Creator designed us. We are indeed "wonderfully made."

Unlimited Access

If we exercise very little, our muscles will become weak. If we exercise frequently, our muscles will grow and become stronger. There is no partiality in this formula. People, who concentrate on improving their muscles, increase in strength. They work day after day and year after year to reach their goals. Other people may envy their results, but be unwilling to match their efforts.

Spiritual happiness also requires persistent effort. Just as heavier weights develop stronger and better muscles, continuing to praise God for difficulties develops a stronger and more joyful spirit. That's the way God designed our spirits to work.

God's formulas for human happiness are easy to understand, but often difficult to execute. Philippians 4:4 says, *Rejoice in the Lord always. I will say it again: Rejoice!* Always? Even when we don't feel like it? Yes! Rejoicing during difficult times is the same as lifting heavy weights in order to strengthen our muscles.

Recently I met an elderly man who had the exuberance of a teenager. He repeatedly and excitedly told me how good God had been to him. When I questioned him, he told me his background.

When he was three weeks old his mother died. To keep him alive his father placed him in homes where he would have food and shelter. The father picked cotton, earning just enough to keep the son alive and enabling him to help whichever family would give board and room to his son. Eventually the son stayed in fifteen different homes. Finally when he was old enough to join his father in picking cotton, they lived together in a one-room shack.

The man explained, "I learned to work in order to stay alive. I learned to appreciate my father's hard work. The more I worked the stronger I became. We stayed poor, and I was never able to attend school, but I grew up being thankful for everything I had to eat or for any small comfort. I'm *still* thankful every minute of the day!"

This man had recently lost the woman he had been married to for fifty-four years. He spoke of her with joy, and thanked God for giving him such a good wife. He expressed no sorrow, or self-pity, and seemed to have nothing on his mind but the good things that God had given him. This man had no idea who I was. His motivation for talking with me was clearly his desire to bless me with his thankful attitude.

Life's experiences can work for or against us. *We* make that decision. When we are old we will continue to radiate the joy, or lack of it, that we are now establishing in our hearts.

I Can Whistle

The thrill of developing a new skill can often launch us to a new and exciting level of happiness. We're delighted by our sense of accomplishment.

When I was five years old I finally learned to whistle. Did I succeed on my first attempt? Alas, no. I had tried and tried, and practiced until, one day a weak "t-w-e-e-t" issued forth from my lips. Success! I remember to this day my elation as I ran to tell my father.

As I grew older I developed and mastered other, more challenging skills. I played the guitar and saxophone, became a competent woodsman, and devised techniques for training dogs to come instantly and happily when beckoned. Each new skill I developed increased my confidence – and joy.

Then came an even more difficult challenge – flying. I'd always had an avid interest in flying, so I enrolled in a flying course. After weeks of demanding instruction I was finally ready (or *hoped* I was ready) to embark on the required solo-flight. Could I succeed in such a new and terrifying endeavor?

Yes, I did succeed. God was my co-pilot as we soared through the heavens and finally brought the plane down to a safe landing. Events can be quite exciting when we succeed for the first time.

Before I could whistle I had no realization of how thrilling the experience would be. Until I was flying alone in an airplane, I could not imagine how that would feel.

There was a time when I had never experienced spiritual joy. I didn't even know it was available. Now

I realize why God's Word says so much about joy. He knew that through Christ we have the potential to have ever increasing joy. But if we have never experienced a joy that *keeps increasing*, we can't understand it, and don't know how to benefit from this free gift of God.

I learned how to whistle by trying over and over. *I've learned how to receive more of God's joy by trying over and over to believe that His joy replaces my unhappiness.* At first I thought I would *never* understand the mystery of being happy in an unhappy world, but gradually and with patience, the hidden joy became mine. Now, when I'm tempted to be unhappy about something, I practice believing that His joy is filling me. And it works! I recommend it!

Stronger Than Gravity

In Ephesians 1:19 Paul says, *I pray that you will begin to understand how incredibly great His power is to help those who believe.* Most of us have failed more than once when we tried to use that verse to solve a severe problem. With all our hearts we longed to believe that God would perform a miracle – but nothing happened. Why? Believing God in such a way that He responds requires patient and persistent development. Like whistling – or flying an airplane solo – we may need practice, practice and more practice. In time our ability to believe God will grow and strengthen. Believing God in small ways is learned first, and, ultimately, greater victories will follow.

Believing God's promises is not passive. It's not for the spiritually lazy. Believing God is active – dynamic! Believing Him changes us, and can change things! Once we strongly believe something, our minds can be almost impossible to change.

Throughout our lives we have actually seen Ephesians 1:19 at work, even when we didn't realize it. How is that? We believed we would not be able to do something, and we were unable to do it! We achieve only what we *believe* we can.

Since Jesus healed the blind and raised the dead, isn't it reasonable to believe He has the power to give us joy? But His joy does not come to those who demand, "Give me joy, and *then* I will believe that I have it." Rather, it comes to those who with child-like faith believe, then say to Him, "I receive Your joy. I have Your joy," and go on to believe it so strongly that their faith controls their feelings.

The Scriptures declare that rivers of living water shall flow from the inmost being of anyone who believes (Jn. 7:38 TLB). When Jesus walked on water He demonstrated that the power God releases through our believing Him is stronger than gravity itself. The universe with its countless stars is controlled by gravity, yet our belief in God exceeds all that force!

You may need to reevaluate your perception of what believing means, and what it can do for you. Remember *how incredibly great God's power is* to help us!

In the Right Direction

When I was flying small airplanes equipped with no radios, I learned painful but important lessons in navigating. I'd point the little craft in the direction I intended to go, but end up miles away from my expected destination. What happened? Winds! Though I couldn't see them, and often didn't even feel them, they blew me in the direction *they were going*.

I've sometimes headed in a direction that I *thought* would lead me into happiness but, to my dismay, ended up miserably unhappy. The "winds" of my own desires moved me in the wrong direction.

It's natural to think that we've followed all the right rules, but the rules just haven't worked for us. We may think, *These rules might help some people, but not me.* Then it's easy for us to rest on our failures, rather than find how we could get moving in the right direction. When we feel miserable, it's natural to believe we've done everything we could to solve our problems, then give up. I know, because I've felt that way too.

But then I began to understand just a little about the faith Jesus talked about. He seemed to be saying that a mountain-sized problem was there for a reason – to help us build mountain-sized faith! I started believing that God would take my mountain-sized dilemmas and use them to work out mountain-sized solutions. And He *did*! Problems can push us in the wrong direction, just as winds can blow an airplane off course. But our faith in God can redirect our course so that we reach our proper destination!

God is on our side, so it's important that we learn to have sufficient faith in Him to get us moving in the *right direction*. Instead of thinking, *this situation is so difficult that I will never find a solution,* we need to think, *God is directing my course*. If you are having difficulty believing that God is actually moving you *any* direction, don't give up – keep believing and trusting Him the best you can, and your faith and trust in Him will grow.

While flying my first little plane I sometimes realized that I was lost. My only recourse then was to study a map and keep going in what seemed to be the right direction. I always found an airport – eventually – but it was my map that guided me. The Bible – God's Word – is our map of life and, when consulted with persistence, will always lead us in the right direction.

God honors our persistence when we strive to believe His promises and to do our best. Persist, and your happiness will gradually increase. You will see that your faith is indeed moving mountains, and moving you closer to God.

Joy is Unchristian

Some folks think it's wrong to place so much emphasis on happiness. They equate joy with a vain, frivolous attitude toward Christian responsibilities. But Psalm 16:11 (KJV) tells us that in God's presence there is *fullness of joy*. Something that is full is – well – full!

Jesus' brother remembered how Jesus dealt with everyday problems. James remembered how Jesus reacted when He cut His finger, fell down or had a disagreement with His brother. James wrote: *Consider it all joy, my brethren, when you encounter various trials* (James 1:2 NASB). He was writing to persecuted Christians who were experiencing really severe trials – yet he admonished them to consider those trials *as joy*! Yes, joy is Christian.

Christianity does seem a little strange. Why would God design a world in which joy could be found in such unexpected places – as in trials? Perhaps God wanted to demonstrate Christ's words, *only a few will find it* (Mt. 7:14). This verse explains among other things, that the road of *unhappiness* is broad, and many will find it, but the road of *happiness* is narrow, and less traveled. But along this road God concealed treasures of great value in unanticipated places. He knew that only determined, persistent people would discover them.

Are *you* determined to find more happiness? You can! Seek God's treasures – seek the good and narrow path, the path less traveled. There will be few walking that route, but what rich rewards you'll find. Be prepared to shed your burdens, though, for this narrow path will not accommodate them.

"But," you ask, "doesn't everyone have burdens?" Yes, they do, but one man's burden is another man's treasure. A man carrying a glittering 100-pound gold nugget from a mine would probably not consider his load a "burden." But if forced to carry a worthless 100-pound boulder, he would likely groan with self-pity. The same weight, but a huge difference in *attitude*.

Mary and I visited a gold mine where a miner showed us a hole in the side of a tunnel that was about three times the size of a football. He said the man who found a nugget in that spot carried it out and never came back to work! I can imagine the radiant smile that he had on his face when he left the dark, dreary mine and hurried toward his new luxurious life. Our burdens (trials) can become our "gold nuggets" as the power of praise takes place in our hearts.

Using Pain for Good

Men of old had time to meditate on spiritual matters much more than we do now. When they traveled from one town to another, they walked, or rode a donkey. When Jesus and His disciples walked from town to town, He had many hours to teach them the important things that are now in the New Testament.

During ancient times David heard in his spirit, *Let all who take refuge in you be glad: Let them ever sing for joy* (Ps. 5:11). As a shepherd, David spent years walking over the hills and valleys of Israel. When he became King David, he was a model of joy. His wife thought it was un-kingly for him to dance in the streets, but David was undeterred. However, joy is not the only feeling that God uses to help us become the happy people He desires us to be. C. S. Lewis wrote, "God uses pain as a megaphone to get our attention."

Pain became an ever-present ingredient in the Apostle Paul's life. Paul wrote that he had a thorn in the flesh that was *a messenger of Satan* (2 Co.12:7). Paul's thorn came after God took him into Paradise, where he saw and heard things that were so awesome he was not permitted to reveal them.

Paul prayed fervently for the thorn to be removed, but it was not. This is the same Paul who had the power to raise the dead, yet God didn't answer his prayer for relief. This suggests, then, that there may be thorns in *us* that will not be removed. Sometimes God chooses to deliver us from our afflictions, but sometimes, in His loving wisdom, He does not. The question then arises: How can I know if God will free me from my thorn – or if He will allow it to remain?

We *do* have one helpful guideline for seeking God's help. If we have carefully asked God three times to remove our thorn, and He has not done so, perhaps He has chosen not to remove it. We can rebel and complain, or we can believe, like Paul did, that God will use it for our ultimate good. So, what are we to do if our thorn – our problem – is not removed? I've answered that question to my own satisfaction. I know that God will always take my problems and use them for my good. Some readers may disagree, but I cling to what I believe God has lovingly taught me.

In 1953 my neck began to hurt as a result of the many times I slammed into the ground after spine-jarring parachute jumps. During three bad landings I was knocked unconscious. At the time, though, my injuries were no big deal for a tough paratrooper. I could get up, return to duty, and forget about it. Airborne soldiers were not supposed to complain about their aches and pains. Injuries were to be carried as a badge of honor.

But the pain didn't go away. It gradually worked its way down my spine and seemed to affect other organs of my body. *But God has used my infirmity to increase my joy!* To some that might seem incredibly strange, but I can attest that I *know* it's true. When standing to speak to a congregation, I often feel guilty. I see so many unhappy faces, yet my own heart is filled with a joy that I can't describe. A delightful warmth surges throughout my being. Paul described this experience in Ephesians, chapter five, as *being drunk, not with wine, but with the Spirit*.

Your thorn in the flesh may be completely different from mine. Whatever your problem, you too may have prayed more than three times for deliverance. You may have been tempted to question God's love for you. Like it or not, you still suffer. Your family and friends may not understand why God hasn't healed you, or fixed your problem. Whatever the cause of your problem, there is an answer. Paul gave it in 2 Corinthians 12:9. *He said to me, My grace is sufficient for you: for my power is made perfect in weakness.* As a result of our right response to our problems, God often increases our joy, giving us greater spiritual strength (see Neh. 8:10).

Overcomers

Overcomers of what? Everything! Excuse me? How could anyone be an overcomer of *everything*?

The word "overcomer" kept coming to my mind, so I knew there was something I was supposed to learn. I knew *I* certainly wasn't an overcomer of *everything*.

The neck injuries I had received as a paratrooper

in WW II have caused me considerable discomfort. Will I allow pain and unhappiness to prevail, or will I – through Christ – be an overcomer? Will I worry about the problem – or rejoice?

As I meditate on the scriptures that pertain to overcoming, I see how many times God chose to use this term. Revelation 21:7 (NKJ) gives us a strong exhortation: *He who overcomes will inherit all things.* All things! Now *that* was the message I needed to see. Perhaps you do, too.

There may be a multitude of things that we have not yet learned to overcome, but what progress toward that end could we make if we really tried? As life piles on the disappointments and pains – physical and emotional – we are increasingly in need of learning to overcome.

One summer when I was a young man, I spent considerable time riding in a horse-drawn wagon while shoveling cow manure on a farmer's fields. I wasn't raised on a farm, so the sight and smell of manure were new to me. It looked ugly and smelled even worse. But the farmer assured me that manure causes corn to grow, and that his corn would feed many hungry people. Imagine that – something ugly and smelly working for good! Now I'm learning that pain is like manure! It can cause good things to grow in us. We don't like having it applied, but it does its work if we use it properly.

There are many reasons to encourage us to learn to be overcomers, but I believe one reason stands out above the others. Revelation 3:21 says: *To him who overcomes, I will give the right to sit with me on my throne, just as I overcame and sat down with my Father on his throne.*

Away With Unhappiness

Neither a prince nor a princess derives any benefit from his or her exalted title if they are stranded in a country where their status is not recognized or honored. They are out of their realm. Christians, too, bear an exalted title – children of God – and they, too, often are given no honor by their fellow men. But their title *is* recognized in the heavenly realm, where both angels and evil spirits know that God is committed to caring for anyone who becomes a member of His family.

But the spiritual realm also knows that God's children are required to believe Him in order to receive His benefits. If God's children don't believe Him, evil spirits can harass them whenever they permit doubts to overcome their faith in God.

The Bible provides numerous illustrations of how God responded to those who trusted Him. Those examples make it abundantly clear that *faith produces results!*

Scripture gives us God's promise that we have the *right* to be filled with joy (see Jn. 15:11). Some Christians have said to me, "I think it's wrong for you to say we should be filled with joy. Many good Christians have terrible problems. You must not understand how painful life can be." These Christians, unfortunately, have believed Satan's lie that problems have the power to destroy our happiness. In fact, God's plan is exactly the opposite. His plan *compels* our problems to work for our good, and can create ever-increasing joy in us! Problems can be used as the ingredients with which God helps us to produce faith. And faith in our loving Heavenly Father always brings joy.

Earth is our training ground. Here we learn to trust

God because of *Who He is*, rather than just the good things He does for us. Hebrews 11:1 explains that *faith is being sure . . . of what we do not see.* In Heaven we will see things clearly, but for now w*e see through a glass, darkly* (1 Cor. 13:12 KJV). With faith and persistence we can learn to trust God to keep His promises, even when we see no immediate results. Once we believe Him, He will release new joy in us. Now is our big opportunity – one we will not have in Heaven!

I was once a perfect illustration of one who translated personal problems into personal unhappiness. I did this for so many years that it seemed perfectly natural to me. And because Christians around me often were mired in unhappiness also, I felt normal. Normal I may have been, but why be normal when God yearns for us to be victorious overcomers? Jesus certainly wasn't "normal" when He faced life. He always persevered, and He prayed for us to have the kind of faith that receives joy from God regardless of our problems. We should pray, then, that we will be like the early believers. Second Corinthians 6:9,10 (TLB) describes them well: *The world ignores us, but we are known to God; we live close to death, but here we are, still very much alive. We have been injured but kept from death. Our hearts ache, but at the same time we have the joy of the Lord. We are poor, but we give rich spiritual gifts to others. We own nothing, and yet we enjoy everything*.

When was the last time you were aware of someone who, "by faith," entered into unhappiness? Probably never – we want to *escape* unhappiness, not enter into it. If we want to escape from unhappiness we must use our faith. Faith is the tool God gives us to rise above what we feel. Faith is our confidence that God *is* doing and will *keep on doing* what He knows is best for us. Faith causes joy to *replace* our sorrows.

Away with unhappiness! Unhappiness is not a product of faith. Up with joy that delivers us out of the clutches of darkness. First Peter 2:9 says, *You are a chosen people . . . a people belonging to God . . . who called you out of darkness into his wonderful light.*

Of what benefit is our title, "Children of God," if we choose to live as if we had no title and no victory in Christ?

Yes, we will be victorious in Heaven. But God has called us to claim that victory now – *today!*

A Secret Weapon

I read a book by a dog trainer that was the funniest book I ever read. Both Mary and I laughed so hilariously that sometimes we could barely read.

I've always wished I could write a book that would make people "roll on the floor" with laughter. But remembering that book has given me a new perspective on joy. The book was funny at the time, but no longer makes me laugh. I can't even remember what most of the funny stories were about. The book gave me *laughter*, but not *joy!*

Laughter is good, and we most likely need more of it, but joy is something that stays with us long after laughter has vanished. Joy from the Lord is like food that "sticks to the ribs" – it nourishes and stays with us when troubles and heartaches strike. Real joy is more like a secret weapon that lies hidden, waiting for the opportunity to strike and destroy the enemy who seeks to afflict us with sadness and tears. Joyful people don't necessarily laugh all the time, but they often laugh when others are in dismay. Joy lifts us when the sky is depressingly black, or the people around us are irritated.

I want to help you acquire more joy. When you

have finished reading this book, I want you to have joy that changes the way you respond to everything, triumphs and trials alike. *I want to be able to do something about your joy: I want to make you happy, not sad.* (2 Cor. 1:24 TLB)

Paul said to Christians who were enduring terrible sufferings, *Always be joyful* (1 Th. 5:16 TLB). My sufferings have been so much less than theirs that I dare not be sad!

Aching Feet!

Your body is engaged in a competition.

As the years go by, your head is trying to hurt worse than your back.

Your shoulders are convinced that they hurt more than your head.

Your hands are competing to see which one can be the clumsiest.

Your knees try to see which one can make the most noise.

Your heart may be saying, "None of you guys could do anything without my help, and I'm really tired."

Your feet are saying, "Listen, up there. I've walked a million miles while all you do up there is relax on top of me." Which will win? Your body . . . or the spirit that lives within?

Our attitudes toward our trials exert a profound influence on our quality of life. They determine whether we are joyful or discouraged. Some folks, having lost their legs, languish sadly behind closed doors, afraid of being seen as cripples. Yet others afflicted with the same handicap venture forth joyfully to compete in wheelchair races. One focuses on the constraints imposed by his handicap; the other on what he can still do. Such is the power of attitude.

Our bodies and spirits are constantly at war with each other, each seeking to control the quality of our days here on earth. It is important, then, to realize that it is our spirits that God uses to create joy in our hearts, not our bodies, and that Satan, the archenemy of happiness, often exploits our physical afflictions to make us unhappy.

All my life I have had feet that ache whenever I am standing. When I was in the third grade, I remember times when I looked for a place to sit, because my feet were hurting. When I was fourteen and had a paper route, I avoided places and customers that required me to walk, and looked instead for those to whom I could deliver by riding my bicycle.

In 1943 I tried to enlist in the Air Force or, baring that, the Navy. *Anywhere* but the ground-pounding, march-intensive Army. Slogging through mud and laboring up steep hills wasn't for me. Too much walking. Too much stress in my tender feet. But, of course, guess where the government put me – in the Army.

And where did the Army assign me? To an infantry outfit infamous for its 10-mile forced marches with full pack and gear and in all extremes of weather. Talk about sore, wet and blistered feet!

But such rigors were merely stateside training. Months later, in combat in Europe, we plodded across what seemed like a million miles of that ravaged continent, and when our boots began falling apart we worried that the enemy could track us by following our bloody footprints. How Satan must have delighted in our discomfort and peril.

When I re-entered the Army as a chaplain in 1953, I thought I had it made. No more ground-pounding, I reassured myself. The war was behind me and I was an officer. I looked forward to a comfortable desk job where my only hiking would be around an office or chapel. But such was not to be. My pleasant illusions were shattered when I was assigned to an Airborne Infantry unit. "Lord," I groaned, "not my will but *Yours* be done. But is this *really* what You want for me?" It was.

Airborne units, the elite of the Army, prided themselves on their superior level of fitness and combat readiness. Their "superior level of fitness," of course, entailed ground-pounding – lots of it! "Why me, Lord?" I groused as I doffed my helmet and wiped away the sweat that ran down my face. "These 25 mile hikes are too much! My pack is cutting into my shoulders and my feet are *killing* me!" Those grueling and all-too-frequent road marches, I must admit, did not instill joy within my heart, and I was not thankful to God for my afflictions. I wasn't happy – but Satan was.

Then, gradually, I felt God working within me. I began to learn an important lesson about praise. I began to see that God was able to take my problem and make it work for my good. Instead of groaning about my hurting feet I learned to praise the Lord for them. I concentrated on believing that He would use them to bless me. Now, every time my feet complain I compel them to march to the tune of "Mary Had a Little Lamb," while I sing, "God is working for my good." Each time I do this I smile with delight, aware of what God is working in my spirit. This helps me to become increasingly glad for *all of God's goodness* to me.

We are all subject to problems that attempt to control our thoughts. Unhappy thoughts can make us grumble and complain. But when we believe that God is always working for our good, He can use even pain to create happiness in our hearts.

What Causes Joy?

"Wipe that frown off your face! Look happy, or I'll slap you!" Sound like an angry, unreasonable parent? Sometimes people read about the joy of the Lord and think God is threatening to "slap" them if they don't smile or act happy. Not so! God isn't interested in a performance. He is looking for people who long for His blessings – people who *want* to have His joy.

Don't ever think that spiritual joy is a "must" before God will give us good things. He sometimes blesses us in order to give us joy, of course, but other times the things He gives us are the opposite of what we want. We always want problems to go away; we always want troubles to end; we always want sunshine to replace darkness. But what does God always want? He always wants us to learn to trust Him. *Without faith it is impossible to please him* (He. 11:6 KJV).

So that's our commission – to trust Him right up to the moment when we think we can trust no longer . . . and then trust Him some more. God knows the joy He plans to give us – we don't. He knows that doubt is our enemy. It was doubt – unbelief – that caused the Israelites to sin, and prevented them from receiving the blessings God had planned for them. God will not honor our doubts, regardless of our reasons, but He *will* honor and bless our faith. We may not want or understand the things that happen in our lives that require our faith to grow. God will let us grumble and complain, moan and groan, until we learn to trust Him. He then uses our trust to serve us large, double-portions of joy. Are you ready to be served?

At one time I was convinced that being a Christian had never provided me with joy. Yet I saw that the Bible promised joy to believers. This was a dilemma to me, so I kept searching for better understanding. Sometimes the solution seemed to be moving further away, and I didn't know what to do but to keep asking God to help me. When I asked other believers why my joy was not as complete as I thought it should be, they sometimes suggested that my expectations were too high, and that we will have joy when we get to Heaven.

Now I'm sure that God's plan is to move closer to Heaven even while we are here on earth. In fact, the more joy we experience here on earth the more we will want to go to Heaven. Exactly what will cause our joy to increase? Praising God! Praising Him for what? *Everything*!

I once spent very little of my time praising God, even when I was praying. There were so many things that I wanted Him to do, and I wanted to be sure I listed them all. And during every prayer I reminded Him of the good things He could do for me. But when I began to learn to praise Him *for everything*, my time with Him became more centered in praise. "Thank You, God, that it's time to get up. Thank You that I'm really tired. I know You will make my tiredness work for my good. And thank You that I have to make this 25-mile-hike today. God, I'm so happy that You are taking care of all these things!"

Praise can become the center of our relationship with God. We will always present our needs to Him, of course, and the needs of other hurting people, but then we will want to thank Him for the confidence we have that He will take care of those needs in His own way. If our attention is drawn back to those same needs, it will usually be to remind God that we are rejoicing in what we know He is already doing. We could continue such rejoicing for hours. Eternity itself will place no limits on our praise to God! The more we praise Him the more radiant our joy will become, and the stronger *we* will feel. *The joy of the* LORD *is your strength* (Ne. 8:10 KJV).

Emergency Room

I was sitting on the edge of the bed when I said, "Mary, I don't remember getting ready for bed." As we get older we often can find ourselves in some part of our home and forget why we went there. Mary said, "Is this something unusual?"

"Yes, it is."

Then I looked at her and said, "Why is your arm in a sling?"

Mary could hear in my voice and see in my eyes that something was wrong. She explained to me that we had been out walking and she had fallen.

When she finished explaining I asked her, "What day was that?" and "What day is this?" Then I asked again, "Why do you have that sling on your arm?"

By this time Mary was frightened. She knew something serious had happened to me.

Only three days earlier Mary and I had been on a happy stroll along a beautiful street near our home. She had tripped and fallen on a cement curb. When she landed, her left shoulder had dislocated and broken in two places. I rushed her to the Hospital Emergency Room where they X-rayed her shoulder and put it back in place. The next day we consulted a specialist who recommended a sling until the bones healed. Now Mary and our daughter-in-law, Ronda, were taking me back to the same Emergency Room. On the way, I repeatedly asked Mary to explain why she had her arm in a sling.

Upon our arrival I was admitted to a room where a long series of tests began. Finally, the tests concluded, the grim-faced doctors informed us that I had a blood clot in my brain. By the next morning, though, my memory had returned! The specialist said I had experienced a temporary memory loss that, he hoped, might never occur again. He told me I was extremely fortunate that I had not suffered permanent mental or physical damage. But something else happened when I was released from the hospital that has had a major influence on my life! The Holy Spirit gave me clear, positive assurance that my recent experience was going to be used by God to accomplish His purpose for me. My mission on earth was entering a new phase.

From the time I was fifteen years old I knew that God wanted me to devote my life to spreading His Good News to people all over the world. With His help we had been able to publish the praise books in forty seven languages, giving them the potential to reach a majority of the people on earth. The praise message had been distributed in nearly every country in the world, and I had also had the opportunity to minister in many of those countries. My heart had sung with joy as I saw His Spirit bring many people to Christ. Now my mission had changed. Now God wanted me to rejoice in His quiet peace so the Holy Spirit could teach me things that I had been too busy to hear. In the following pages you will read some of the new things I have been learning.

Understanding God's Heart

A million-dollar secret is "hidden" in the Bible, right in the open where many do not see it. *I am bringing all my energies to bear on this one thing: Forgetting the past and looking forward to what lies ahead* (Ph. 3:13 TLB).

We came into this world crying, in case you don't remember. We cried when we wanted milk . . . or for any other reason that caused us unhappiness.

We grew up complaining about anything we didn't like. That's the nature of fallen man. We complain without realizing what we are doing, and usually can't even remember that we have done so. Being thankful for what we have, rather than pining over what we don't have, can be very difficult for us. Changing our natural human tendency to complain requires a BIG effort. So, why should we change? For our own good!

It's imperative that we strive to understand – really understand God's purpose for us – to learn to trust His loving wisdom as He allows trials to come our way. When we entertain unhappy thoughts about things that we *don't have*, we may lose what we *do have*.

God had provided abundantly for Adam and Eve, but they wanted what they *didn't* have. We know the tragic results.

The Israelites, too, didn't have everything they wanted, but God had delivered them from slavery, provided them with abundant food, gave them clothing that never wore out and, best of all, planned a glorious future for them in the Promised Land. But they kept dwelling on and complaining about what they wanted, rather than what they had. We can want what we don't have one hundred times a day, and not even realize it. But if we do, we may suffer a penalty.

I had an operation to improve my vision. The procedure was a success and my sight was wonderfully corrected. At first my thoughts were centered on how blessed I was. But then a thought came to me: *But my vision isn't as good as it was when I was young.* As soon as I entertained that thought, my joy began to decline. I'm thankful I had learned to recognize such negative thoughts, and thus was able to focus my thoughts again on how good God has been to me. A happy heart enjoys what it has, and does not dwell on what it doesn't have. God wants His church to be a thankful people. *You* can be a thankful person, and when you are, you will reap *many* rewards.

We have many opportunities to wish that we had more money, friends, intelligence, free time, health, beauty, skill . . . the list could go on and on. But when we concentrate on and are thankful for the good things that we do have, we move closer to God's heart. His Holy Spirit will warm us with His comfort.

God's Aid to a Happy Marriage

Joy is not an exclusive luxury that God designed to benefit a favored few; rather, it is a tool that He designed to assist everyone who believes Him. It is joy, for example, that helps a spouse to keep a bright, happy spirit when the other is unkind. Without joy, an unhappy spouse is quick to strike back at any perceived mistreatment – which creates even more strife. Joy doesn't automatically create perfect marriages, but it *does* have the power to dissolve marital strife, and greatly enrich a marriage.

Joy helps us deal effectively with children, neighbors, employers – as well as with anyone who has the knack for stirring up trouble. Joy doesn't make us perfect, but it is a wonderful tool that helps us solve problems.

The Christian who has inner joy has resources to defeat the most menacing threats against his happiness. This gives him the freedom to look at difficult situations and calmly devise solutions. A happy person can get out of a car with a flat tire and smile at the three tires that are not flat.

Joy is like a warrior's shield, a shield designed by God to protect us from many troubles. Without that shield we are far more vulnerable to the problems of everyday living.

When I was a Private in the Army I had no control over what was on the menu at any meal. I ate what was set before me, or I went hungry. That lack of control often made us privates quite unhappy. We were free to express our dissatisfaction, of course, – but . . . never to anyone of higher rank! Someone of higher rank might growl, "Okay, you go on KP tonight and wash all the pots and pans." Such a lack of control results in frustration and unhappiness.

But everything changed when I became a Lieutenant Colonel! Now I had more control. Now Mess Sergeants quickly responded to any requests that I made. Now when I entered a Mess Hall I had no anxiety, and I never had any reason to be angry. Increased control over our lives often gives us increased peace of mind.

Now I have control over things that previously would have made me unhappy. This control is not the result of an elevated rank or status. Rather, it is a direct result of the joy that God has helped me to receive. Now when nasty things happen, I rejoice as I think of the good solutions God may impart and what I should do while I wait for Him to act.

Good Predicaments

The small task in our yard promised to take only a few minutes to complete – ten at the most. I was in a hurry, but thought this would be something I could do quickly – then move on to more important matters.

Ten minutes stretched into twenty, and every part of the chore went wrong. Some of the tools wouldn't work. Others broke. Trip after trip to my tool chest caused the clock to keep moving forward. My frustration increased, and I felt like quitting.

Do you care how long the project took me? No, I know you don't. In fact, I was the only one who cared how long it took. Even God didn't care, but He must have been amused by my impatience. God could cause every worthwhile task in the world to be completed quickly and with no hassles. But we are not called by God to accomplish *things.* God is interested in the changes He wants to see *in us.*

The Bible tells us, *Do not be anxious about anything* (Ph. 4:6). And *that, an anxious heart weighs a man down* (Prov. 12:25). Why, then, do we so often choose to be anxious and weighted down?

One of the most important reasons for our being here on earth is for us to learn to appreciate the peace of heart and mind that Jesus paid such a high price to provide us. Jesus wants and expects us to complete our daily tasks, of course, but His *first* priority is for us to become the worry-free people He wants us to be. With that in mind, then, our daily chores become opportunities for us to examine our attitudes and responses toward our problems. Why be stressed out over things when we don't need to be? If that sounds "super-spiritual," think of it this way: Why hurry through life to accomplish things that in eternity will amount to nothing? Why not learn to perform our daily tasks with *attitudes* that are pleasing to God?

The more we learn not to be anxious, the easier and less strenuous life becomes. We may still have the same problems, the same tasks to perform, but the feelings of drudgery and frustration will no longer control our thoughts. Once we have changed our attitudes, we will soon develop a quiet confidence that God is doing something good in us. Ultimately, that "something" is exactly what we will need when really difficult problems arise. I look forward to learning the new things that God wants to teach me. It may take me a long time to learn, but I'll be an eager student!

Confidence Regarding Family

Believing that bad things are going to happen can be just as effective a use of our faith as believing that good things will happen. Faith, then, can be a double-edged sword. It can be applied *for* us or *against* us.

I had always thought of faith as a tool that helps us receive good things from God. It does, but in time I realized that this same force, if applied improperly, could exert equal power to bring us the very things we *don't* want. Consider Job 3:25 (KJV): *The thing which I greatly feared is come upon me, and that which I was afraid of is come unto me.* Job learned the hard way that the sword of faith, if wielded improperly, could smite him. We can learn from Job's ordeal. If we believe that someone we care about is headed for certain disaster or an unhappy life, we are exercising our faith – but in the wrong way!

God often lets us be in a position where there is nothing we can do to prevent loved ones from making mistakes. But He has given us the opportunity to use our faith in whatever way we choose. We can refuse to permit our expectations to be based solely on the evidence that we *see.* Instead, we must base our expectations on what we resolutely *believe*.

For example, we know that God has forgiven our sins, even though we may not be able to present concrete evidence that He has. We know we're forgiven even if we cannot see in ourselves the results of our confidence in God's grace. We may not see any evidence that God is working good in our loved ones either, but we can trust that He is, and with this confidence comes blessed peace of heart and mind.

We may not be able to explain it, but we know it is true.

A hurting person may declare, "But I've been believing for *so long*. It's exhausting to keep on believing, without evidence, that things will get better." But they *should* say, "The length of time I've been believing means that much *less* time I have to wait for God to reveal His solution!"

We may ask ourselves "What did Peter accomplish in his effort to prevent Jesus from going to Jerusalem where He would be arrested and killed?" Absolutely nothing. Regardless of his well-intentioned motives, Peter's fears only caused him to receive an extra-painful rebuke from Christ.

You and I may invite a similar rebuke if our doubts keep us from trusting God to help our loved ones. We may feel that we are justifiably worried about them, because we love them, but that does not excuse our failure to trust God.

Regardless of what other people may tell you, place your confidence in *God's incomparably great power to those who believe* (Ep.1:19).

Unlimited Opportunities

Jesus brought healing and joy to many people. Would you like to talk with the ones He healed? Maybe they could give us some good advice on how to receive more good things from Him. Here is some of the advice they might give:

1. Ask Jesus to touch you. When He touched me I was instantly healed and received great joy.

2. You don't need to ask Him to touch you. Just touch His clothing and you will be healed.

3. All you need to do is cry out to Jesus long and loudly, and He will heal you.

4. The best way to receive healing is to have Him

spit on some dirt and then place the dirt on you.

5. Find friends who will cut a hole in the roof and lower you to where He is present. Then He will heal you.

Why did Jesus use so many different methods to help people? I believe He wanted us to understand that He works in people's lives in the unique ways that are best for each of them.

Jesus wants *you* to experience His power in special ways. Never be discouraged because He doesn't work in your life the same way that He works in someone else. Permit Him to work in you in *His* way and in *His* time.

Jesus knew that faith in God could accomplish anything. What is the "anything" you would like Him to do for you? Whatever it is, it isn't difficult for Him to do, but first He often wants to make changes in us that will cause us to not be impatient, troubled, or afraid.

Maybe we can't step right up and be joyful in the midst of difficult things right now, but we can learn. And we need to begin learning now, *right where we are*. I learned through simple everyday things, like not being troubled when a traffic light turned red, or when my car wouldn't start. Later, as I learned to praise God in more difficult situations, the greater my joy became. Now, I look forward to learning how I can be happy in other situations. Ultimately, our opportunities to grow in joy are unlimited!

Being Successful

Albert Einstein said, "Do not worry about your difficulties in mathematics; I can assure you that mine are even greater." His statement puzzled me, but then I heard a man who is eminently successful in his own field say, "The more successful I've become, the bigger the playing field seems to be. I have more goals I'm trying to reach now than at any time in my life."

Being successful in any endeavor opens new doors to us. For example, if we study the planets and stars that we can easily see, we might soon expand our desire to learn more about the entire universe. Even though a child in school is initially puzzled by all the words he needs to learn to read, once reading is mastered, the potential of what he can read and enjoy is endless.

It has been said that the best way to stay mentally young is to keep learning. Likewise, we can say that the best way to stay young at *heart* is to keep learning how to give thanks and praise to the Lord.

God created in us a desire to obtain joy. He even built our bodies in such a way that they require happiness in order to be healthy. Regardless of your state of health, though, you can improve your well-being by learning how to possess inner joy.

If we are unhappy about an irksome predicament, solving that problem will not be the end of our troubles. New difficulties will inevitably come along, and sometimes those difficulties are even more severe. Until we learn the remarkable ways that God has provided to give us peace of mind, problems will always overwhelm us.

The solution to problems with marriage, children, finances or health is always the same. Faith. Faith that God is working through Christ to help us in our present situation, brings, *God's peace, which is far more wonderful than the human mind can understand. His peace will keep your thoughts and your hearts quiet and at rest as you trust in Christ Jesus* (Ph. 4:7 TLB). I urge you to believe that "God's peace" is now causing your heart to be "quiet and at rest."

Always Filled With Joy?

Am I always filled with joy? I wish I were! Since I've been a Christian, there have been times when I had very little joy. Those dark periods were quite stressful and lasted far too long. But as I began to understand more about God's wonderful plans for His people, I learned that I could let the Holy Spirit banish my unhappy thoughts.

When we get to Heaven we will have perfect joy, but for now most of us have times when we continue to wrestle with unhappy thoughts. I too have struggled with unhappiness, but now I rejoice in how much God has helped me to change from my old ways. The longer I live and praise God, the easier it becomes to throw off thoughts that try to steal my happiness.

If unhappiness is frequently a part of your life, I strongly recommend that you seek new understanding of how to receive God's solution. I assure you that you'll be glad, and God is well-pleased when we find ways to experience His happiness!

Don't simply acknowledge your unhappiness, but then make no effort to find the solution. A big secret is to believe that God is changing you. Believe that God is doing a great work in you. It is not an unattainable goal for God to change you into a cheerful person. Trusting Him to do this is the most practical and effective way for you to become the person God wants you to be. Many, many people have told me they were once abjectly miserable, but have now, because of their faith, become remarkably happy. Their joy has grown more than they ever dreamed it could!

Revelation 22:17 (KJV) says, *Whosoever will, let him take the water of life freely*. Ponder the meaning of "whosoever will." Whosoever means anyone can partake of God's freely given blessings. So when you feel unloved, ill, unsuccessful, betrayed, or ignored, don't surrender to unhappiness. These are the very times when we must believe that God gives us the water of life freely. *These are the very times to remember that God who started this great work in you will keep at it and bring it to a flourishing finish* (see Ph. 1:6).

Learning to Be Content

When Christ was born, the angel told the shepherds that Jesus was coming to: *bring good news of great joy to all men* (Lu. 2:10). We might prefer that this "great joy" be given to us without our having to do anything, but God grants His joy to those who *believe* Him. Believing is not as easy as we would like it to be, but God requires our faith before He will change us and impart His joy to us. We should believe, then, that He is waiting to give us happiness right now, wherever we are, whatever our situation.

If we had an opportunity to question Paul, we might ask him, "Why did you persist in praising God despite being laughed at, beaten, imprisoned and otherwise persecuted for your beliefs? Your life was much more difficult than mine, yet you said you were content, whatever your circumstances. Why did God give you such a special gift of contentment?"

Paul might answer, "I never said that God had given me any such gift. Look again at Philippians 4:11, where I said *I have learned to be content whatever the circumstances*. God did not bestow a special gift upon me, neither was my contentment a reward for my service to Him. I *learned* to be content in small things, and then in bigger things until, eventually, I was content in *all* things"

The angel announced that great joy was coming

to *all* men. Since God wants you to have this gift, it is important that you *learn* to receive it. Of course, we can still get to Heaven even if we are grouches, but there may be many people who do not make it to Heaven, because we did not do our best to demonstrate the great joy that Jesus came to give us.

In church we might present ourselves as happy, loving, kind people. But it's crucial that we learn to be happy loving and kind around our family, fellow workers, neighbors and casual acquaintances! By doing this, we will become the people that Jesus said we should be. We can believe that God gives us His happiness, and the best time to receive it is now.

Our Solution

The people of Israel – are united against Jesus, your anointed Son, your holy servant. They won't stop at anything that you in your wise power will let them do (Ac. 4:27-28 TLB). The enemies of Christ could do anything that God permitted them to do. With God's permission they humiliated, tortured and killed Christ. They also murdered many of those who believed in Him. The early believers accepted God's right to allow evil men to do evil things, but they were firm in their conviction that whatever God permitted, He would cause to work for their good.

It's very easy for us modern Christians to accept the idea that God would never give us problems. However, we must not embrace such false notions of what *we* think God should do. God speaks for Himself: *I form the light, and create darkness: I make peace, and create evil: I the Lord do all these things* (Is. 45:7 KJV).

The Hebrew word *ra,* is translated here as *evil*. It is also translated as distress, misery, injury, calamity, adversity, disaster as well as other words that are merely unpleasant. That's quite a list of things that God says He sometimes creates. We should not pretend, then, that these things are not of God. They are, so we must strive to understand His words, since they were written for our benefit.

It gives me great joy to know that God can take evil and *compel* it to work for our good. Folks who fail to understand this suffer real turmoil when they strive to reconcile how God could be all-powerful, yet permit so much misery to exist in our world.

We can confront even severe problems and know that God will use them to perfect His will in us. *God is at work within you, helping you want to obey him, and then helping you do what he wants* (Ph. 2:13 TLB). If we believe, then, that "God is at work" within us, our happiness will keep growing regardless of our trials.

Running With Joy

An apple a day keeps the doctor away. That proverb may or may not be true, but one thing is sure: For an apple to benefit us, we must eat it. Likewise, the joy of the Lord will never help us unless we do something to receive it into our hearts.

If we feel unhappy, it may seem a little silly even to try to believe that happiness can replace our sorrow. Believing, after all, isn't as easy as eating an apple! Eating is something we understand, believing is not. We can, however, *learn* to believe. I'm learning to increase my believing through diligent practice. Practice, of course, requires persistence and patience, qualities that are evidence of the Holy Spirit's work in us (see Gal. 5:22). In Luke 11:9 Jesus urges us to be persistent: *Keep on asking and you will keep on getting; keep on looking and you will keep on finding.*

Jesus told His disciples to *receive the Holy Spirit* (Jn. 20:22). Sometimes, when feeling sad, I've practiced believing that Jesus was at that moment urging me to receive the Holy Spirit in fresh newness. And as I believed Him, my joy increased.

Sometimes while I'm walking I practice taking "steps of faith." Second Corinthians 5:7 (KJV) says, *We walk by faith, not by sight,* so I practice believing that with each step I'm receiving more of His joy. Quite often, by the time I finish my walk, I feel like *running* with joy!

Find ways to administer faith and joy to *your* heart. If one way doesn't help you, try another . . . and another. If unhappiness has persistently ruled some part of your life, it may not give up easily, but it can be replaced – with *joy*.

Building Our Ark

We believe that Jesus performed miracles, but we may find it difficult to believe that we too can do things that seem impossible. How, for example, can we muster the faith to rejoice when our problems grow increasingly severe? We can because God gives us that ability.

I had an operation to remove calcium spurs in my shoulder. The therapy for my recovery was excruciating, but during that time other agonizing problems developed until I had seven infirmities at the same time! My ability to rejoice was sadly depleted, you can be sure – until a beautifully clear picture came to my mind. I saw the wonderful product of Noah's trust in God.

God chose an ark as His means to save Noah and his family from the flood (see Gen. 6). Building such a huge vessel where there was no place to float it was a big stretch for Noah's faith. As he worked, each day must have seemed harder than the day before. There was no evidence that a flood would *ever* come; yet for 100 years Noah obeyed God. He kept working and kept believing. Then, when the rains came and the ark began to rise, I saw how the same waters that brought destruction to so many others, brought life to Noah and his family.

You and I face problems that could easily discourage us if we did not know how to rise above them! Jesus is our ark, sent by God to lift us above our problems. Problems that could overwhelm us if we don't believe that God can make them work *for* us. I keep learning more about the joys of placing my confidence in Him, regardless of how difficult the situations might be. I experience new happiness as I picture myself rising above my problems!

When we are frustrated by problems we usually do not want God to tell us to trust Him. We want Him to *do* something. But just like Noah, God has us here to learn to trust and believe Him.

We can trust God even when there is no outward evidence that our faith is accomplishing anything. Sometimes the longer we have to trust Him the more difficult it is to keep clinging to our faith. But none of us have to trust God for 100 years as Noah did. Just as the ark saved Noah and his family, Jesus will lift *us* up above our problems. That confidence gives me joy.

God is Our Sculptor

I've sometimes wished I could write a book that would be replete with elegant phrases and masterly crafted words. A silly desire? Yes, I know it is, but within all of us is a secret desire to be something above and beyond what we are.

God, our Creator, sees these desires and wants us to approach Him and say, "God, You made me exactly the way You wanted me to be." Then as we accept ourselves just as we are, we can enjoy life even while being aware of our shortcomings! Other folks may criticize our weaknesses (and probably will) but we can smile to ourselves as we think, *Just wait until you see what God plans to do with me.*"

A cold and lifeless lump of clay is unimpressive to look at, but its malleable nature makes it an easy substance to shape. A skilled sculptor, his fingers working deftly, can transform that lifeless lump into a thing of exquisite beauty that can endure for many years.

You and I can be likened to a lump of clay that God, the Master Sculptor, wants to shape. Be assured, though, that when God shapes us we will be infinitely more precious than anything devised by mere man, and that His work of art will endure not for years, but for eternity.

So don't despair at your inability to be like someone else. God fashioned you with meticulous care to be a *totally unique creation*, a happy and contented creation that unbelievers will see and want to emulate.

Take a reality check. Does your life radiate the kind of joy that God, your Sculptor, wants to instill in you?

Enjoying Boring Work

A task that is boring to one person can be a good way of earning a living to another. I've worked in steel mills, foundries, sawmills, printing shops and a food packing plant, where employees did the same work year after year. During those years they had developed a camaraderie that enabled them to enjoy working together to earn their living. However, my thought was, *I want out of here!*

What is boring to one person can be exactly what another person *wants* to do. The task is the same, but there is a difference within each person that causes him to react to that task in a different way.

We can even learn how to bring about a change in our attitude toward our work. How can we do that? We can believe that God is using our employment to instill the discipline and refinement that we need. God is responsive to everything we do and is especially interested in anything that will inspire a positive change in us. He could easily arrange a different assignment for us, but why should He if He designed our employment to fit exactly what we need?

Rebellion over our chores in life is actually rebellion against God. Rebellion displeases God, but when we find joy in our work, home, church and community activities, we please Him. As you can see then, our potential to find joy in our circumstances is unlimited.

People who can find happiness in whatever they are doing usually have happiness in their hearts. Look, then, for ways to find happiness in everything you do, while others seek reasons to be unhappy in nearly everything they do.

In our home I took on the responsibility to do a certain job that needed to be done every day. It wasn't the sort of work I enjoy, and I thought most men would feel the same way. I tried to not complain, but in my heart I was thinking, *I sure wish I didn't have to do this.*

One day I sensed the Holy Spirit asking me if I thought God wanted me to perform that task. What could I say? Of course He must want me to do it. So why wasn't I enjoying the opportunity to do what God wanted me to do? I had to stop and ponder that question.

We may think it is asking too much of us to enjoy something we *don't* enjoy, but now I understand that the task itself was not my problem. The problem was within me. Without intending to, I had made up my mind that I didn't enjoy my chore, and had steadfastly stuck to that decision. But could I work at changing my attitude? I could, and I did. I started declaring my gladness that God had:

Given me the strength to do it.

Given me the materials to work with.

Given me a home in which to work and loved ones to work for.

Given me a spirit that could be guided by His Spirit.

On and on I expanded my reasons for being glad. Within a few days something wonderful happened within me. I was able to find joy in my unwanted task. My new success blessed me, and I was clearly aware that God was pleased, too.

Now I encourage you to think about the tasks that God has arranged in your life. Do you want to find joy in them? You can! At first such a goal may seem too difficult to reach, but don't give up. God sometimes arranges boring work so we will have the opportunity to increase our spiritual strength. Enjoy your challenge!

Chosen For Heaven

Have you been chosen for Heaven? You should be intensely happy if you believe God has actually chosen you (see He. 3:1).

Who are these chosen ones? *We who . . . now have the same Father he* (Jesus) *has* (He. 2:11 TLB). Incredible! Amazing! Pause a moment and meditate on who you are.

Study the book of Hebrews, and see that these

blessed persons are those who believe in Jesus as their Savior.

When I think about Jesus as my Savior, I sometimes experience such joy that it seems as if I could never be unhappy again. Please don't wait until the trumpet sounds before you enjoy the blessings Christ has given you. Above all, don't be an unhappy complainer. The Israelites *complained against him in the desert while he was testing them* (Heb. 3:8), and they ended up in serious trouble. You and I will be tested too, of course. We will be tempted to be unhappy, and sometimes we will complain. But if we concentrate on the incredible gift of eternal life God has given us, our happiness *will* steadily increase.

Journey to Bethlehem

Christmas can be a happy time if we don't think about Joseph and Mary's difficult journey from Nazareth to Bethlehem. They traveled ninety miles over rugged, mountainous terrain while she was heavy with child. We usually don't think of how Mary felt as she endured all those miles of difficult riding or walking beside a donkey.

If we had stood along the rough trail and watched as they passed, we would not have sung, "Joy to the World." More likely we would have thought, *Why is God so unfair to Mary?* Or, *Why doesn't God send a chariot to make it easier for her?*

We celebrate Christmas as we do because we see the end result of it. We picture Jesus as already born, and the angels proclaiming to the shepherds the *good news of great joy.*

God wants us to celebrate our own difficult journeys through life in the same way that we now celebrate Christmas. He wants us to believe that our journeys are as certain to end in victory as was Christ's!

If we look with eyes of faith, we can see reasons to celebrate. We can see that God is with us, providing exactly what we need in order to fulfill His plan for each of us. We acknowledge our sufferings, but see the coming victory as far too important for us to concentrate on our painful journey. God inspired Paul to write, *We do not lose heart . . . for our light and momentary troubles are achieving for us an eternal glory that far outweighs them all* (2 Co. 4:16,17).

Our troubles *are* "momentary", and God promises to make them achieve an eternal celebration! God asks us to prove our faith in Him by beginning our happy celebration NOW.

Increasing Confidence

Do you want to learn how to gain more confidence in God?

Consider parents teaching a child to walk. The baby tries, but lacks confidence and falls. The parents urge the child on. From the child's perspective it would be natural for him to think, *All you want me to do is fall down and hurt myself again.*

I've never seen parents walking back and forth in front of their baby, saying, "See, this is the way you do it." No, they urge the child to do it himself. The child needs to keep trying until he gains more strength and confidence. That is the only way he can ever learn to walk.

It would be easy for you and me to say to God, "Please show me how to have more confidence in You. I've tried, but I keep having doubts. I keep falling down." But God, our loving Father, knows that we need to keep trying.

The baby will never have enough strength to walk until it practices resisting gravity. Although gravity may seem to be an enemy, it is actually designed by God to help our muscles become stronger.

Doubt tries to drag us down and defeat our confidence in God. But it can be overcome, and as we win our struggles against doubt, our confidence in God grows.

Jesus urged His disciples to have more faith. On one occasion He urged Peter to muster his faith and walk on the water. Peter had undoubtedly jumped into the water many times before, and gravity had always pulled him under. But now, something about Jesus' confidence convinced Peter, and this time he actually walked on the water!

Then what happened? Peter saw the high waves; lost his faith and his confidence in Jesus – and down he went. (I wonder if Jesus ever gave him a refresher course).

On another occasion Jesus gave the Disciples baskets containing small amounts of bread and fish and told them to feed thousands of hungry people. Their confidence in Jesus may have been tested, but they obeyed – and there was more food than they needed.

Jesus told the Disciples that He would be killed, but then promised that He would be resurrected in three days. That was too much for them. They knew He was able to raise the dead, but could He raise Himself from the dead? And why would He even be killed if He were the Messiah?

Confidence is always difficult to have when things we don't understand are involved, but God has told us to rejoice in Him always (see Ph. 4:4). That's a reasonable and easy command to obey when life is going fairly well. But what about the stormy times –

times when the waves are high and the sea is churning? Can we rejoice in Him then? Yes, we can. Think of these times as something like gravity that pulls a child downward. Hard times, like gravity, can force us to grow in spiritual strength and confidence! God understands this, even if we don't.

To help us along, God has provided the Comforter to live in our hearts (see Jn.15:26). We can trust Him to provide the comfort we need. And believing that creates joy — ever increasing joy.

Something New

The earth was without form, and void; and darkness was upon the face of the deep. And the Spirit of God moved (Gen.1:2).

When anything is "created," something new comes into existence.

When we have experiences that give us fear, anger or sorrow, that is the time to ask God to create *something new* in us. Our circumstances may seem to be without purpose, and be as dark as the world was in the beginning, but the Creator of the universe can easily change them. Or He can change us.

We need to remember that our earth was changed from being dark and void when *the Spirit of God moved.* When God moves, He can change and create something new!

People frequently have difficulty accepting the idea of praising God for "all things" (see Ep. 5:20), because their understanding of God is much too limited. But God is not limited. He can take something that seems worthless and hopeless, and change it into something new and valuable. He does this every time a person is born again! God takes bad people and makes them into a new creation (see 2 Co. 5:17). We would be foolish, then, to doubt His almighty power to do whatever He knows needs to be done. We do *our part* when we trust His promises. Trust God to create something new in you and your confidence in Him will give you ever-increasing joy.

Some folks squander endless energy worrying over why God permits bad things to happen. That is the same as asking why God created the world *without form, and void.* Why didn't He create it right to begin with?

Why should we waste our energy worrying over things we don't understand? God did what He wanted to do, how He wanted to do it, and when He wanted to do it. He works exactly the same way today. He permits painful things to happen to us, and gives us the opportunity to trust Him.

The creation account is a beautiful object lesson for us. First came things that were dark and void – things without any apparent good purpose or value. Then God changed those things into that which was new and good. If you trust Him and believe His promises, He will change what He feels needs to be changed in your circumstances and in you. Once you understand this principle, you are freed from endless stress, and can receive new peace of heart and mind.

Using Our Opportunities

You who are going to destroy the temple and build it in three days, save yourself! Come down from the cross, if you are the Son of God! (Mt. 27:40). Think of the joy that would have exploded in the hearts of Jesus' followers if He had come down from the cross! Instead, He stayed there as if He had no power, and as if the disciples were not pleading with God to do something.

Since God did nothing, the unbelievers mocked: *He saved others, they said, but he can't save himself! He's the King of Israel! Let him come down now from the cross, and we will believe in him* (Vs. 42).

Perhaps nothing can be so devastating to us as to feel that God is ignoring our prayers. We may become discouraged, and have the empty, hopeless feeling that since God isn't helping us, there is no reason to rejoice.

Where is God when we hurt? Why doesn't He help us? Why is our faith so weak that we are unable to receive good things from Him when we need them the most? These questions can plague our minds to distraction until we decide what we really believe about our God.

Satan questioned Eve about God's integrity. Was God being fair with her? he whispered. Eve listened. Then Adam listened. And the results were *disastrous*.

You and I hear the same voice: "If God is with you, why doesn't He do something to help you?" Once we succumb to that line of reasoning, our inner turmoil mounts. *Why doesn't God help me?* we cry. From that point on we can often descend into complete despair.

Think about the words Jesus' enemies used to taunt Him, and it will be clear that they actually came from Satan. With that insight, we will be much better prepared to "hang on our cross" with the same calm confidence that Jesus had.

Jesus knew that His purpose on earth was to fulfill His Father's plan for Him. This plan, though, seemed unacceptable to His disciples and to others who loved Him. God's blueprint for you and me may also seem unacceptable to others, but, like Jesus, we too have the opportunity to proclaim, "Not my will, Lord, but Yours be done."

Most of us understand that it was Christ's mission

to die on the cross to purchase for us the gift of eternal life. But Jesus also saw His life as an opportunity to do *whatever* God wanted.

Life presents us with many opportunities to question God. We can fail to trust Him, and question why He allows our painful circumstances. Or we can choose to trust Him in all things and reap the reward of joy, both now and for eternity.

Genuine Feelings

Do happy Christians sometimes cry? Do they ever endure times of deep sorrow? Do they ever feel as if they could never laugh again?

Yes. Yes. And yes. Christians are, after all, only human.

A loving father feels no criticism when his hurting child cries. His first instinct is to hold and comfort the child who is upset. The father wants to do whatever he can to relieve the distress. But if the child is throwing a temper tantrum, the father has a far different attitude.

I believe that God sees us, His children, in a similar way. If we are genuinely hurting He understands and wants to comfort us. But if we are merely complaining because we resent His failure to do what we want, He sees that we need appropriate discipline.

Be assured that God *always* knows why we are unhappy, and that He comforts or disciplines us according to the attitude of our heart.

Hearing God

Imagine that you were having a really bad day. Imagine that you were unhappy about something that someone had said or done to you. Or perhaps *you* were at fault, and were feeling guilty and miserable about something you had done to someone else. What if you just didn't feel well? What should you do? Should you continue to suffer, and let unhappiness prevail? Why not do something to banish your despair? But what?

The cause of depression is often our failure to follow God's instructions – His plans for us. God wants us to be victorious over our feelings. He knows that people will fail us, but He wants His Spirit to control *our reactions*. People never control our response to what they do, but how *we* react is of paramount interest to God! If one minute from now you should die, you will face *God,* not the people who give you trouble. It is God who has told you to rejoice always, and to Him you must answer.

Have you tried to hear God speak to you when someone or something has upset you? If you haven't, you're missing a great blessing. You can learn to hear Him. If the only thing you ever hear God say to you is, *I love you,* or, *I will take care of this situation for you,* just those words alone can fill you with enormous happiness!

It's true that people sometimes think they hear messages from God, but are listening for the wrong things. They think God is telling them that they will have great wealth or power, or success. But these are not the messages we need to hear or believe. What we *need* to believe with all our hearts is that our Creator loves us, is with us, and is meeting all our needs in the exact way He knows is best.

You may one day find yourself in a situation in which you think no one really cares about you. That is when you will need to be *really sure* that God Himself loves you, and is working for your good. Learn to listen

61

to God – *really* listen – and He will change your sadness into gladness!

What Faith Can Produce

Tiger Woods, the champion golfer, said that the only way he could win a tournament was to have *faith* that he would win. This insightful statement from such a prodigy in his field should be an inspiration for us to exercise our faith in the things *we* do. Faith, after all, is a necessary ingredient for success in any endeavor.

Understand that God *wants* you to be happy, and is involved in every detail of your life. Trust Him, then, and you will find peace through your steadfast confidence in God. This confidence assures you that no accident, earthquake, tornado, hurricane, flood, fire or lightning can touch you unless God uses it for your good. No calamity – no bacteria, disease or other affliction has, *in itself*, the power to destroy you. Hardship can come to you only if God in His infinite wisdom allows it. You, a child of God, are under His care as surely and completely as if Jesus were here in the flesh, standing by your side. Surely that knowledge should give you joy! Have faith in Him, and step-by-step, moment-by-moment, you can grow more confident of God's involvement in your life.

Faith in God gives us peace in the midst of anything that life can throw at us. Anything! Being in a den of lions was not conducive to peace of mind, but Daniel said angels came and closed the lions' mouths! (see Dan. 6:22).

Early Christians were at peace as they faced violent death in the arena, a peace that caused amazed spectators to marvel at the calm composure of the doomed but steadfast believers. What a witness they must have been! What a testament to their faith in God!

Faith in God brings us peace that overcomes stress, strife, depression and turmoil of all kinds. What great happiness can be ours through faith in our Lord!

This overcoming faith that overpowers every ordeal that can ever come to us, is God's gift to anyone who puts forth the effort to trust in and rely on His Son.

When Does He Control?

Just as we rely on Christ to provide us the gift of eternal life, there are other circumstances in which God also wants us to depend on His Son. Jesus said: *All authority in heaven and on earth has been given to me* (Mt. 28:18). To what extent, then, does Jesus use His authority to control events here on earth? Is it seldom? Frequently? At all times?

Our faith in Christ should declare that He has, and uses, His dominion over anything He desires to control. How you and I understand and respect His power determines how we view all of life.

Some folks live under the misguided assumption that Satan has more power here on earth than Jesus has. They live in fear of the evils that may befall them. But if we believe that Christ forgives our sins and gives us the gift of eternal life, why not believe that He is in control of and has jurisdiction over *everything*?

Since I started trusting Jesus in more areas of my life, I have experienced greater and greater happiness. I understand now that He has total control over everything that happens to Merlin Carothers. It has become clearer to me, too, that He wants to accept whatever burdens I will bring and leave with Him.

Why should we worry about what might happen to us as long as Jesus is in control? Why should we fear sickness if we believe that He created, and is in charge of our bodies? Ultimately, why should we fear *anything* at all?

It is with enthusiasm that I urge you to surrender all jurisdiction to Christ. Not only will you find happiness and great peace of mind, but you will also please God.

For many years I worried about things that never happened. During that time, I had little understanding of the total authority that God has given to Jesus. Even though I knew Jesus had invited us to, *Come to me, all you who are weary and burdened, and I will give you rest* (Mt.11:28), it somehow didn't seem to work in my life.

But when I began to appreciate Christ's eagerness to accept my burdens, I grasped that He wanted to give me peace, rest and refuge. And my happiness began to increase.

You, too, may be struggling under heavy burdens. If so, rejoice that you have the opportunity to surrender them to Christ. Let Him take charge of your fear, your pain and your heartache. Then trust Jesus to work them for your good. Easier said than done? Yes, but persist. Believe that Christ exercises ultimate control and will always do whatever He knows is best. The more we accept that, the easier every part of life on earth becomes.

As we learn to rest in Him, happiness permeates and dominates every part of our lives.

Digging For Diamonds

Finding joy in our physical suffering, or in other severe problems, can be difficult.

If someone you trusted gave you a shovel and promised that you would find a diamond somewhere beneath your feet, would you dig for it? How deep?

Philippians 4:7 (TLB) tells us: *You will experience God's peace, which is far more wonderful than the human mind can understand. His peace will keep your thoughts and your hearts quiet and at rest as you trust in Christ Jesus* (Vs. 7).

Recently I needed to walk up a steep hill, but I was extremely tired, and my body groaned that it couldn't go another step. But then I remembered God's promise always to supply whatever I needed. *He will supply all your needs from his riches in glory because of what Christ Jesus has done for us* (Vs. 19).

I thought, *What do I need to do to benefit from this promise?* Then it came to me. The answer to my question was the same answer that Jesus gave the blind men. He said to them, *Because of your faith it will happen* (Mt. 9:29 TLB). And they were healed.

So I believed that Jesus would give me the strength I needed, and acted on that belief. As I made a determined effort to walk as if I was bursting with youthful strength, my exhaustion quickly faded, and up the hill I went. It was then, as I walked briskly upward, that I experienced Isaiah 40:31: *They will run and not grow weary.*

Please don't misunderstand me. Usually when I'm tired, I know it's because I need to rest. When we need rest, *that* is precisely what God wants us to have. What we need is the wisdom to know the difference.

If we believe, and persevere, Christ will accomplish within us and through us whatever He feels is necessary.

A Major Cause of Unhappiness

All of us dislike some things that are part of our lives. Wealthy people, for example, may once have been confident that riches would make them blissfully happy. Then, when happiness continued to elude their grasp, they may have thought, *I would be happy if I didn't have to pay so much tax.* Or, *If I could regain my health, then I would be happy.*

A major cause of unhappiness is that so few of us have learned that for every action there is always a consequence. Sex outside of marriage produces unhappy consequences – many of them. Overeating or drinking produces unhappy consequences. Unwillingness to work or to save money produces unhappy consequences. The world is filled with unhappy people. Unhappiness is nothing new. It has been around forever.

Happy people are *unique.* They may be surrounded by unpleasant people and things, but are still happy. That's one of the reasons the angels were so joyful about the birth of Jesus: God was going to introduce amazingly Good News to the world. Peace and joy were to be made available to people who were miserable, despised, rejected, in prison, hungry or cold. This joyous news introduced a new revelation of God's Will for all mankind.

The greatest tragedy of life is not our unhappy world. It is that so many of us have not yet understood the fabulous Good News! So many of us are still afraid to believe that a loving, perfect, all-powerful God could take all the circumstances in our lives and *force* them to work for our good.

God designed Christ's death and resurrection to prove His point. He took the most evil thing that Satan could ever do – the crucifixion of Jesus – and forced it to work the greatest good that has ever happened on this earth – our opportunity for salvation. God wanted you and me to see that there is NOTHING He can not do. And He challenges us to believe Him. It's our decision. We can follow Jesus' example, and believe that God is in perfect control of all things, or we can be miserably unhappy in this wretched, chaotic world.

My own life has been enormously blessed to see the radiant faces of the people who excitedly rocket upward in their faith, stand up on the inside and declare, "I believe that God is working for my good. I will rejoice and be glad!" Their excitement and joy is always a wonder to behold.

If My Situation Changes

I have had the pleasure of training a number of dogs. In some ways dogs can be remarkably similar to us. They can get ideas ingrained in them that are very difficult to change. For example, if their mother is fearful she teaches her brood to be afraid.

Many people have learned to be afraid or worried. If we talk to them about becoming a happy person, they may respond, "I'm unhappy because of what someone has done to me." Or, "If my situation changes, then talk to me about happiness." No matter how many reasons a person has to be happy today, he may still cling to the possibility that things may get bad *tomorrow*.

We would all exhibit the same apprehension about our problems if it were not for what Jesus did for us. He said, *In this world you will have tribulation; but be of good cheer, I have overcome the world* (Jn. 16:22 NKJ).

No matter what has broken our hearts, it is something Jesus came to heal. He may or may not change our situation, but He *always* wants to help us have His joy. If I can convince you of that one point, your life will be changed forever!

Training and More Training

A Seeing Eye dog is a marvel to behold. A patient trainer has altered nearly every basic instinct of that noble creature. A blind person, after all, must rely on a dog that has been trained to ignore most of its natural instincts.

Dogs love to do whatever they want to do; and, if allowed to run unrestrained by discipline and training, will obey their natural urges. When the dog encounters another dog, or its scent, his instinct compels him to investigate. Instinct governs nearly every aspect of a dog's life – that's his nature.

But these natural instincts must be drastically changed if the guide dog is to be the eyes of his owner. The trainer uses every conceivable opportunity to remold the way this dog thinks. Day after day, and month after month the trainer and dog go everywhere that a blind person might go. The dog is compelled to focus on nothing but the person he is leading. He makes hundreds and even thousands of mistakes. At each session the trainer makes the in-training animal follow the prescribed behavior. After countless hours and corrections, the dog eventually becomes one of the famous and beloved Seeing-Eye dogs. By this time he enjoys his duties, and is ready to become the joy and savior of his master.

You and I are born complainers. It is our nature and life-long habit to be troubled about many things. We have practiced the dubious art of complaining tens of thousands of times, and have learned a multitude of reasons to be unhappy. Then, in our Bibles we read rather astonishing verses that tell us not to be troubled (see Jn.14:1). This takes us aback, and can seem almost impossible to obey. Some folks become so discouraged that they simply give up and ignore Christ's words. They lack persistence.

We can gain some valuable insights into persistence from the training of the Seeing Eye dog. Wouldn't it be foolish and shortsighted to give up on the dog if after just one month he didn't understand what was being asked of him? We humans are more complex than dogs, and require *even more* training. We are more set in our ways, and require far more convincing to give up our habit of being troubled.

Each of us has chosen our own reasons to be troubled and unhappy. In time, these reasons become deeply ingrained in our thoughts and feelings. The very words, "be filled with joy," can anger or confuse us, because unhappiness has become such a strong habit in our lives. Giving up such a long-held habit can seem to be anywhere from not worth considering to downright impossible.

In 2 Corinthians 5:17, we see that when we become Christians, we become brand new people inside. Does that mean our old, anxious natures are immediately changed too? Does that mean that we will never be troubled again? No, it doesn't, because that isn't the way God planned to work in us. God works in His own ways His wonders to perform, and it is through our troubles that He teaches us to be happy and at peace.

We will make many mistakes, but Jesus, our patient and untiring Shepherd, is always there to help us try again. He knows that we are being trained to be God's happy, obedient children.

When in prison, hungry, cold, hated by men, the early Christians sang songs of joy. Those who heard them saw that they were a new variety of human being. Then new Christians took up the same challenge and taught the next generation what it meant to have

a song in their hearts no matter what their circumstances. And when they were about to be fed to the
lions, they filled the arenas with song. What "Seeing
Eye" examples they were to us!

Saved From the Environment

The cars that zoomed by seemed to fill the air with
poison. Wait a minute, why did I think of poison? There
have been cars around me all my life, and I had never
thought of them poisoning me.

Oh yes, now I remember. I had heard on the radio
and television, and read in the newspapers, that cars
are emitting deadly poisons. And so, there I was,
reacting in fear to what I had been told.

Then I shifted my attention to my heavenly
source of news, and was reminded that there has
always been a far more dangerous source of pollution
on earth – pollution of the soul. Men die eternally from
that. Sin has polluted the souls of men since man first
rebelled against God.

Now the good news. As God's children, we are no
longer under the curse of sin and its pollution! I walked
beside the speeding cars and thought to myself, *I'm
God's son. Nothing in this world can rob me of Christ's
joy. Whether I live or die is in His hands.*

What freedom and deliverance we have in Christ!
We do not have to fall prey to the sin pollution of this
world. What happens around us need not control the
life that God has given us through His Son. We can
sing, shout and laugh because we are protected by
God's love for us. The more I understand this, the
happier I become.

God's children live under *His protection.* Let the
world live in fear if it so wishes. As for us, let us trust
God to protect us just as He protected the Israelites

from the dreadful plagues that came upon their Egyptian captors! Whether we live or die is *in His hands.* It's not only unnecessary for us to worry about things that may or may not happen to us, but it's also an effective way to undermine and squander our happiness.

Replacing Unhappiness

Every day we make at least one hundred decisions to be either *happy or unhappy*! If the habit of unhappiness is well developed within us, we can decide to be unhappy without even consciously thinking about it.

Repetition of unhappy thoughts causes them to become deeply ingrained in our minds. Eventually we even *look* like an unhappy person. When asleep, we may have distressing, unhappy dreams. Even the organs within our bodies can function and churn to the tune of unhappiness.

If the above description sounds like you . . . don't distress for you can change, and I am living proof that it is possible. Of course it takes an effort to shift from an old way of thinking to a new way. People who try to do this on their own often give up trying. We need to remember this very important fact: *The same power that raised Christ from the dead, is the power that will help us change: Just as Christ was raised from the dead through the power of the Father, we too may live a new life* (Ro. 6:4 TLB).

Of course, it takes something powerful to change us. Christ's resurrection from the dead demonstrated the same power that God wants to use to help us (see Eph. 1:19,20). If we have had unhappy thoughts for many years, it may seem ridiculous to suggest that *we have been choosing them.* We may have decided long ago that our *circumstances* are what dictate our feelings. If that were true, Paul would have been one of the most unhappy persons who ever lived. But Paul chose to be happy, because he believed that joy was his inheritance in Christ.

Instead of just passively accepting unhappiness, you and I should concentrate on learning to receive the triumph that Christ has offered us. Consider the joy of having Christ working in you in every situation, whatever it may be! Christ did not permit the situations around Him to control His reactions to them. No matter what happened to Him, He was victorious. Such a life may seem utterly impossible for mortals like you and me, but we can strive to be mirrors that brightly reflect the glory of the Lord. *And as the Spirit of the Lord works within us, we become more and more like Him* (2 Co. 3:18 TLB).

If we have no objections to becoming more and more like Christ, then we should accept the challenge to let the Spirit of the Lord work in us. He will work in us to make us the happiest people on earth. You are a prime candidate to be a mirror that actually reflects the new way of living that Jesus came to demonstrate. What potentials we have to become *more and more like Him*!

Solution For Unhappiness

A voice within me said, "Merlin, your happiness or unhappiness depends on what *you believe*." That was hard to understand, since my unhappiness often resulted from other people's actions and from situations I couldn't control.

Even after examining the scriptures, it was still very difficult for me to understand how my own happiness depended on what I believed. My old habits were hard to change, but I kept remembering: "Merlin, your happiness depends on what *you believe*."

Jesus frequently encouraged His followers to believe that God would provide the things they needed. But we have been taught in our culture to believe that if we have enough confidence in *ourselves* we can do anything. That attitude may seem to work for a time, but eventually we hit a stone wall. Confidence in *self* is not what Jesus was talking about. He urged us to have confidence in *Him*. Paul understood that, and wrote: *I can do everything God asks me to with the help of Christ who gives me the strength and power* (Ph. 4:13 TLB).

Paul went on to influence the world for Christ perhaps more than any other person who has ever lived. Since that time, Christians have learned that when they depend on Christ they really *are* able to do things that previously seemed impossible.

Even if right now we don't have sufficient faith to "move mountains," we can exercise the faith we *do* have. Whenever unhappiness steals into our hearts we can practice believing that Jesus gives us the *strength and power* to resist gloom and depression. Then unhappiness loses its control over us. This doesn't mean that an immediate surge of happiness sweeps through us, but gradually, day by day, we will feel His transforming joy rising in our hearts.

Just how far can we go in believing that our joy is increasing? Much further than we are! You can believe right now that God is helping you to be a little happier than you have ever been.

Regular, persistent exercise strengthens our muscles. In the same way, our happiness increases as we persist in believing that God is helping us to be the happy people that He wants us to be.

Accepting the Invitation

Jesus told a parable about a man who had sent out invitations to his banquet. *A certain man was preparing a great banquet and invited many guests* (Lu. 14:16). Some of those who had been invited gave weak excuses to explain why they couldn't attend. *I have just bought a field, and I must go and see it ... I have just bought five yoke of oxen, and I'm on my way to try them out ... I just got married, so I can't come* (Vs. 18-20).

The man who had sent the invitations said, *I tell you, not one of those men who were invited will get a taste of my banquet* (Vs. 24).

Through parables, Jesus taught us many principles that we can apply to every area of our lives. His parable of the banquet warns us not to preoccupy ourselves with trivial, worldly affairs that cause us to miss receiving God's free and eternal blessings.

If we focus our attention and interests exclusively on our own affairs, we can fail to receive the gifts that God offers us. For example, in John 17:13 Jesus said: *I say these things . . . so that they may have the full measure of my joy.*

Jesus' parable further explains that the happiness one person fails to accept will be given to someone who really wants it. You and I can step forward and receive what others have rejected!

No matter how valid a person's reasons for being unhappy may seem, God has invited us to receive Christ's joy. If you have been making excuses about why you haven't accepted His invitation, lay them aside, and declare that you now receive the *full measure of His joy*.

Eyes That See

I knew my eyesight wasn't as good as it used to be. I needed more light to read the fine print. But I wasn't prepared for what the eye doctor said.

"Your right eye has a cataract that needs to be removed."

After leaving the doctor's office, I covered my left eye, and to my surprise I could barely read! But my left eye could read even the fine print. Then I tried reading the same print with both eyes. It looked exactly the same as it did when I used only my left eye. For months I had been reading with only my left eye, and hadn't noticed how weak my right eye had become!

Then I concentrated on the fine print with both eyes, and tried to determine what my right eye was seeing. I couldn't! No matter how hard I tried, all I could see was the clear vision of my left eye. What did I learn?

For weeks I had tried to think of a new way to illustrate how important it is for us to have joy regardless of our circumstances. We *choose* how we look at the challenges that life brings us. We can look at events through eyes of faith and believe that God is working out something for our good. Or, we can look at our circumstance and doubt that God is doing anything.

We learned years ago to "see" life from one point of view or the other, and we accept our way of seeing things as perfectly natural.

If you have been failing to see God's special care over you, try closing your "weak eye" and see your life as Jesus saw His. Jesus believed that God would accomplish something important through His suffering. The disciples couldn't understand His point of view until after His resurrection. Then, they too, began to see His death and resurrection as God's plan to work great good for all mankind.

Later the doctor removed the cataract from my eye and remarkably improved my sight. Trusting God removes the cloudiness that prevents us from seeing the good that He is now working in and for us.

Are You a Failure?

Have you ever felt as if you were a failure? Cheer up. Nearly everyone has felt the same discouragement at one time or another.

Those who are wealthy and powerful, or are gifted with health and beauty, often feel as if they are just as much a failure as the average person does. Why would this be? It is because they face the same demons that the rest of us do. These evil spirits are always whispering, "You aren't good enough, and you never will be."

God has wonderful plans for His children, but He also knows the difficulties that we face. He is not worried about our *failures,* because He knows our *futures*. We could say that He has "read the last page." He wants us to see ourselves as His handiwork – His diamonds in the rough that He is making into precious sparkling jewels.

We do not belong to ourselves. We need to understand that we are God's creation. God is molding us, and He does not design failures! His children are victorious because of what *He has done*. Look at yourself as God describes you in 2 Corinthians 5:17 (TLB): *When someone becomes a Christian, he becomes a brand new person inside. He is not the same anymore. A new life has begun!*

This transformation is not something *you* have done. Nor is it something you have earned. It is God's gift to you in honor of what *Christ* has done! What an awesome incentive for you to be happy!

God designs each new Christian with unlimited potential. But our enemy, Satan, does not accept this as a "done deal." He tries to convince us that what Christ has done for us does not entitle us to be victorious. Satan knows that if he can deceive us into clinging to our old defeatist attitude, we will be discouraged and not likely to have the faith that we need. After all, if we have faith we can accomplish anything. And that would make us dangerous to our enemy.

When we have the assurance that God is working *in* us, as well as *for* us, we can then confidently trust Him to fulfill His good plans for us (see Je. 29:11).

God *with* us, working *in* us, doing His will *through* us. What a wonderful and powerful way for Him to help you realize that your life *is* worthwhile. Because of Jesus, you are not a failure, and are assured of living with Him forever.

My Failures

I received a message that drastically changed the way I think about my failures. I hope it will also change the way you think about yours.

I often judged myself harshly for failing to be the person I thought I should be. Our desire to be better people can be painful, and can make us quite unhappy.

In my spirit I heard, "Merlin, if God judged you for your mistakes and failures, He would declare you a far worse person than you have ever realized."

Ouch! That hurt! What hope did I have if God saw me as more of a failure than I saw myself? What a radical change this made in my thinking! I couldn't possibly see my mistakes and failures as clearly as God sees them. If I were ninety-five percent blind, would I be qualified to examine a piece of cloth to see if it is soiled? If not, why should I spend my time suffering over my deficiencies if I can see only a tiny part of them?

Upon what, then, should we focus? On God's forgiveness and grace! We know that *Christ died for sins once for all, the righteous for the unrighteous, to bring you to God* (1 Pe. 3:18).

If you believe that by God's grace you are forgiven, you have no excuse for being unhappy about your failures. Place your confidence, joy and happiness in Christ and in *His goodness*. Your joy can be in Him, and in what He has done for you. The more you rejoice in Christ's goodness, the more He will work His perfect will in you.

Falling in Love

Fortunate men and women have experienced the wonder of falling head-over-heels in love. The feeling that causes rockets of joy to burst within them, is something to be remembered and cherished. I have presided at many weddings, and the happiness proclaimed by radiant smiles is a joy to behold. But romantic love too often turns into dislike, even hatred. Why? What went wrong? Where did all the joy go?

God built within us His formula for the survival of the human race. Boy meets girl, they are attracted to one another, they want to get married and have a family. So far, so good. But in time, the initial attraction can easily fade away. It has served its purpose. Once they are married, they must learn to live in harmony. They must decide if they will love and honor one another no matter what life thrusts upon them. If they make selfish choices, they may eventually seek other romantic encounters which will also eventually lose the romantic joy.

The joy of a permanent marriage is a matter of choice. Through right choices, a new kind of pleasure evolves. The couple works at helping, forgiving, encouraging, enjoying and understanding one another. Blessed are the husband and wife who find happiness in living and being together through "thick and thin." An unbreakable bond is developed that helps them face the hardships of life together.

But there is another blessed union that has even greater potential. It is that between a Christian and Jesus.

Those who daily choose to trust in, rely on, and follow Jesus, experience a bonding with Him that creates ever-increasing happiness.

Family Problems

Family relations can be wonderful – or disastrous. We want our families to believe that we always desire what is best for them, but they don't always see it that way. Have you noticed?

They love you, then sometimes shun you. You may be clueless about what is bothering them; or, you may understand, but don't know what to do about it. Families can lift us to heights of great joy – the gurgling babies, active toddlers and venturesome teenagers. The brothers and sisters, aunts and uncles, parents and grandparents. We cherish fond memories of graduations, birthdays and weddings. We love our families immensely. But as we love them, we open our hearts to being hurt.

What, then, should we do when we are hurt?

Should we get angry and cling stubbornly to our hurt feelings? Not if having peace and joy in our hearts is our objective.

Our best and most powerful response to family strife is to believe that God will always use it to work His good *in us*. If we really believe that, we are "home free."

We should stop fretting about family members' attitudes towards us. Whether they are good or bad, God can cause them to change. Our only task is to leave all such "heavy duty" matters to Him. That leaves our hearts free to rejoice in His perfect care.

In the meantime, God will honor our faith and take care of our families in His own time and in His own way. That way we get to be about our assignment to rejoice in Him at all times and in all situations.

Feel First?

If I do not *feel* happy, contented or delighted, why should I *act* that way? That's a logical and all-too familiar question. Most of us:

Want to feel happy first.

Believe that we have to have a reason to be happy.

But happiness that comes from God does not depend on how we happen to feel. We may feel miserable because we are ill or have physical infirmities or for a variety of other reasons. But God does not want us to limit our happiness to only those times when we feel good. Feelings pass away. The joy of the Lord is very different, and is what all of us urgently need. How can we obtain this joy? We must learn to believe that it is ours, through Christ

Nehemiah 8:10 says: *The joy of the Lord is your strength.* We can read this verse, quote it – even sing it. But God's words cannot change us until we *believe them.* We must believe that the written words of God are true, and able to change us. His joy is something we can receive if we determine to do so. Learning to believe may seem difficult, but it is well worth the effort it takes. We want God's joy. We need it, and in some difficult situations we cannot survive without it. So again, what should we do? Practice believing.

Practice saying, *The joy of the Lord is my strength.* Repeat this verse until each word comes to life for you. If necessary, repeat it one hundred times, or until its message has your full attention. Practice believing that it is working in you. Exercise that faith throughout the day. Use it especially when you are upset about anything! Practice this whether you *feel* like it or not.

What results should you expect? An increase in faith. Faith that is exercised will grow; then God's joy will permeate your thoughts and gradually *control your feelings.*

Exercise Your Spirit

Jesus told the disciples that His soul was *overwhelmed with sorrow* (Mk. 14:34), and asked them to pray. Then He went a short distance and prayed with His face to the ground. When Jesus returned, He found the disciples sleeping. He said to them, *The spirit is willing, but the body is weak* (Mt. 26:41).

I had always thought that Jesus was lamenting the weakness of the disciples' flesh. Now I believe He was emphasizing that merely having a *willing* spirit is not enough if we want to obey His commandments.

After Pentecost the disciples continued to have weak bodies, but their spirits began to grow in strength until they were eager – *afire* to serve God. They were infused with a new and dynamic power –*the Holy Spirit.* From that point on, they embarked on a fervent crusade that wonderfully and powerfully changed the future of the world.

Like the disciples, you and I are "weak of flesh." And like them, we are fallible and will succumb. But, like them, we too can receive power from God.

Most people would agree that the older we get, the weaker our physical bodies become. That may be true, but take heart: some Christian seniors give us wonderful hope when they tell us that their *spirits* have become stronger!

When the disciples became sleepy, they succumbed to their flesh and slept. Their spirits were willing, but were not strong enough to resist. The disciples' weakness demonstrated that mere *willingness* to serve God is not enough.

Like your muscles, your spirit grows stronger the more it is exercised. One excellent way to exercise the spirit is to allow it to control what you do! Instead of attending church, praying, reading the Bible, helping others, or being cheerful just when you *feel like it*, decide *what you should do* – then *do* it. Then the Spirit of Christ will work the same kind of wonders through you as He worked in the disciples. The disciples were frail, fallible average men, but when they accepted Christ's invitation to be filled with His Spirit, they accomplished the "impossible." They changed the world. Through Christ, you too will be able to accomplish the impossible.

Rapid Results

I sometimes eat a certain food that has been recommended to me as being extra healthy. Recently I was asked if the food did me any good, and I had to admit, "I don't know. I just try to be healthy by doing things that I hope will be good for me."

But there are some things that we can *know* whether or not they are good for us. For example, if you put into practice the principles that you read in this book, your spirit will be strengthened. How long will it take for you to benefit? Not long!

When we believe that God is working for our good, we often see surprisingly rapid results. And the more we *practice* believing, the more rapidly the results can come. It's a little like building a wall. The higher it gets, the higher we will be if we stand on top of it. But if we build walls of unbelief, then it becomes increasingly difficult to believe that good things are coming.

The fact that you are reading this book indicates that you are open to believing God for new things. Believe that God desires to do new things in you. Believe that His goodness is what motivates Him to do *good in you*. The moment you believe Him for some new good thing, may be the very moment you feel a stirring within you that you have never before experienced. You may feel more at peace, more joyful. Only God knows what you really need, so He ignores the misguided desires of your weak flesh and moves in ways that will delightfully surprise and bless you.

I've sometimes been happily astonished by how quickly my state of mind is changed when I believe God is doing something good in me. The oppressive weight of my negative thoughts vanishes as if a heavy stone has been lifted from my heart.

Believing for good things is such a powerful way to change the way we feel. Jesus expressed surprise that people found this truth so difficult to understand. The moment we believe Jesus is in control of our lives, is the moment He works in new ways to increase our happiness.

Blessed Assurance

We want to KNOW that our spouse loves us. Without that certainty, a marriage can be a very unhappy union.

We want to KNOW that our boss plans to keep us on the payroll. How unpleasant it would be, to expect a pink slip every day.

We want to know the clear status of all the things that are important to us. I feel sorry for those who believe they will never know *for sure* that they are going to Heaven until they actually get there. I pray that you will be excited about the certainty of what Jesus has accomplished for us. I mean *really* excited!

No matter how hard we might try, we will never *know* that we are going to Heaven *if* we believe our destiny depends on our *own* goodness.

God says he will accept and acquit us – declare us "not guilty" – if we trust Jesus Christ to take away our sins. And we all can be saved in this same way, by coming to Christ (Ro. 3:22 TLB).

It is from God alone that you have your life through Christ Jesus. He showed us God's plan of salvation; he was the one who made us acceptable to God; he made us pure and holy and gave himself to purchase our salvation (1 Co. 1:30 TLB).

Herein lies our joy! God wants to give us Christ's righteousness and let that righteousness be as if it were *our very own*! What a miracle! What a cause for excitement and ever-increasing happiness for the rest of our lives! What a pity it would be to have been offered such assurance and not take advantage of it!

In Every Church

A conscientious pastor is alert to any indication that his people are disobeying God. On Sunday mornings he feels compelled to warn them of the dangers they face. But in his concern, he may neglect to tell them the Good News of the Gospel. In time they may forget what it is. In many churches I have asked people to raise their hands if they were positive that they were going to Heaven. To my dismay I have often seen uncertain, confused responses.

God's Good News should be a central theme in *every* church. Mark 16:15 (TLB) says: *He told them, You are to go into all the world and preach the Good News to everyone, everywhere.* If we are thoroughly convinced that God's plan is *good*, we should be eager to help others know what it is.

Picture the twelve disciples leaving Jerusalem and preaching their message to the rest of the world. What did they tell people? What caused Christianity to spread throughout the world? The disciples told people that through faith in Jesus they could receive the free gift of Heaven. This was exciting news to them! They had never heard such a message, and it may surprise you to know that many people around you have never heard or understood it either! Think of the opportunities we have! What a wonderful gift God has given us – we can be used by Him! When people ask me the polite question, "How are you today?" I sometimes reply, "I feel wonderful. Would you like to know why?" What can they say but "Yes" when they have initiated the conversation? Then I say, "I feel wonderful because I know I'm going to Heaven." Sometimes they will say, "How do you know that?" When they do, they have opened the door for me to share the best news that we have ever heard.

That's the way God designed His plan to work, and why He wants to give us His *exceedingly great joy*.

Why This — Why That?

Christians are always being pulled toward the same tragic mistake that caused Adam and Eve to be cast from paradise: doubt in God's goodness. We are inevitably drawn toward that same sin by the same Evil One who tempted them. It worked with them, so he thinks *why do something different*? How often have you been tempted to doubt God's goodness toward you? How often has the thought entered your mind, *If God is really working for my good, why is my life so difficult? Why this? Why that?* The same old temptation, but always clad in a variety of disguises to deceive us.

One of God's simple instructions to us is that we are to trust Him. That's all – just *trust Him.* Adam and Eve weren't required to comprehend His will, and neither are we. God requires only that we trust Him.

Why should we trust God? Because He is powerful enough to have created us? Not at all - I see no reason to trust Him because of that. We should trust Him because of our confidence in *His goodness*. If we are to have increased joy and peace, we must have increasing faith in His goodness.

God is perfectly able and willing to supply every-thing we need, each moment of every day. The more we believe this and trust Him, the more real His goodness *towards us* becomes.

In Psalm 31:19 (TLB) David says: *Oh, how great is your goodness . . . For you have stored up great blessings for those who trust and reverence you. The more strongly we believe this, the happier we become.*

When We Grumble

For my own benefit, I had incorrectly interpreted Philippians 4:4 to mean, "Grumble in the Lord always, and again I say, grumble." Those were the bad old days.

What I didn't understand then was that I needed a completely new attitude, as in: *Be made new in the attitude of your minds* (Ep. 4:23).

Instead of being "made new," our minds can sometimes be influenced by the negative attitudes of others around us. We may hear, "The weather sure has been terrible," or other complaints about the way God chooses to run His universe. That's somewhat like complaining, "If I were God, I would do better." Such an attitude undermines our trust in God. As our trust is reduced, so is our happiness.

So why not rejoice in what God is doing, whatever it may be?

When we are born again God puts something in us that is a little like an orchestra. When we grumble, the instruments get off key – with sour notes. When we rejoice, the instruments begin to tune up, and when we keep rejoicing, a symphony begins in our hearts.

So tune up *your* orchestra. Whatever you are doing and wherever you may be, say to yourself "I rejoice in the Lord." Keep repeating this declaration, and with increasing enthusiasm until you feel a joyful transformation taking place within you. Is this change psychological? Physical? Perhaps a combination of both? I'm not sure, but I know that I step with a renewed vigor, and a joyful new song plays in my heart, a song put there by God Himself. King David heard it, and it caused him to dance joyfully before the Lord. Since then, multitudes of Christians have rejoiced in this song of joy, a song that you, too, can sing as the Spirit of God enters and changes your heart.

Great Joy — NOW

Being joyful is often a matter of our perspective.

Planning and thinking about a coming vacation is often a substantial part of enjoying it. The more unusual and exciting the vacation, the more anticipation we feel while making our preparations.

Planning for and thinking about Heaven is the most exciting sense of anticipation we can ever feel. Jesus knew this when He told us to *leap for joy, because great is your reward in heaven* (Lu. 6:23).

The joyful expectation of Heaven gives some Christians great happiness, while other Christians seldom even think of Heaven. I believe it is vital that we frequently meditate on our eternal home.

Jesus was happy about His coming return to His Father, because He knew the glories that awaited Him. Throughout history Christians have reported visions in which they saw into the next world. Their absolute certainty of Heaven gave them joy even while they were still here on earth.

I encourage *you* to learn more about Heaven. Consult your Bible—it refers often to the joys that will be ours there. Revelations 7:16,17 and 1 Peter 1:4 provide especially thrilling descriptions of our eternal home that will inspire you with ever-increasing anticipation.

Several years ago God granted me a glimpse into the outskirts of Heaven, a glimpse I described in my book *From Fear to Faith*. What a vision! What I saw gives me great joy every time I meditate on it. My joy increases whenever I further contemplate God's plans for our eternity. When I face a difficult situation I sometimes concentrate on what we already know about Heaven: *God shall wipe away all tears from their eyes; and there shall be no more death, neither sorrow, nor crying, neither shall there be any more pain: for the former things are passed away* (Rev. 21:4 KJV).

These promises from God should give us great joy – now!

Heaven – What a Place!

What ignorance clouds the minds of those who say, "Heaven must be boring with all that singing and praising God. Too much like going to church all the time."

Our Creator has created Heaven with everything that can possibly bring us joy. Everything! First Corinthians 2:9 says, *No eye has seen, no ear has heard, no mind has conceived what God has prepared for those who love him.* In Heaven we will continue to develop our capacity to enjoy what God is now preparing for us.

Many of the joys we've had on earth may be amplified in eternity. Think of learning to play a musical instrument, painting a beautiful picture, studying the universe, writing masterpieces for others to enjoy, causing others to laugh – and possibly even learning new things for all eternity!

An all-powerful God can easily prepare a Heaven that will fully satisfy us, His children, whom He created in His own image. Isaiah 35:10 assures us that *everlasting joy and gladness* will be ours, and that *sorrow and sighing* will be no more.

It makes me happy to recognize that our Creator is a God of JOY. It is His *nature* to want us to be happy, and He wants to be with happy people! In Heaven we will experience *exceedingly and abundantly* more happiness than we have ever thought possible!

We Can Do It!

Long before the first telescope, long before astronomers and philosophers pondered the marvels of the sky, and long before men had any comprehension of the vast number of stars in the universe, God whispered a secret to David. David wrote, *The heavens declare the glory of God; the skies proclaim the work of his hands* (Ps. 19:1).

Even up to the twentieth century, men believed that the total number of stars equaled only a few thousand, and astronomers had no idea the immensity of each star. Possibly to ancient observers God's creation was not something at which to marvel.

Even though David had little understanding of the universe, the Holy Spirit revealed to him that the heavens revealed the glory of God.

Now we know that just our own galaxy with its 400 billion stars stretches across more than 80,000 light-years (One light-year being about 6 trillion miles!). The star that is nearest to earth, Proxima, is actually four light-years away! The furthermost galaxy that can be seen by the Hubble telescope, is ten to fourteen billion light-years away! This, plus the billions of known galaxies of the universe, reveals a great deal about God's glory. Yet skeptics who cannot understand even the complexities of our earth, doubt God's existence! Worse, even we Christians sometimes doubt God's power to keep His promises.

When I catch myself wondering if God will do all the things the Bible promises, I reflect upon the marvelous things He revealed about His creation to David.

There must be many reasons to rejoice that we have not thought about yet. For now, let's live and act as if we believe that God's glory deserves our obedience to His command that we *Rejoice and be glad, because great is your reward in heaven* (Mt. 5:12).

We can do it!

Free as a Bird

I learned a helpful lesson while watching a bird gaily hopping along a fence. It seemed to be having such fun, and I thought *I'd like to be able to bounce about on a fence with such beautiful grace.* But I guess I'm too heavy for such fun things.

Jesus understood that our problems are often "too heavy" for us. In Matthew 11:28 He said, *Come to me, all you who are weary and burdened, and I will give you rest*.

We sometimes feel so overburdened by our problems that we can't manage them. They seem much too heavy for us. The solution? Get rid of our burdens. Sounds good, but how do we do it?

Jesus' solution is simple: Come to Me, and I will take care of your problems. But did He understand what real life is like? Yes, He certainly did – think of some of the problems Jesus encountered.

When the raging storm threatened to sink the ship – He told the storm to be still. There was no food to feed thousands of hungry people – He supplied the food. People were lame, blind or deaf – He healed them. Even the dead posed no problem to Him – He simply called them back to life. The people Jesus healed must have skipped home feeling like that little bird I saw hopping along the fence. They too could run and leap with joy. When we feel stressed or burdened, we should remember those people, and ask the Lord to help us delight in that same freedom.

Jesus carried complicated burdens that we will never be asked to bear, plus the ordinary hardships that have always afflicted humanity. He had no home that He could call His own, one of His friends was murdered, and His friends failed to help Him when His life was threatened. But during all His experiences He was always confident that God was with Him. He was free. And He has offered you that same freedom and unfailing confidence. They are His gifts to you if you will trust Him.

I urge you to accept Christ's gifts of freedom and confidence now. Set down your burdens and let Him carry them. Then I invite you to recite this prayer: Jesus, today I place my confidence in You. I will trust You to carry my heavy burdens. I receive in my heart the joy and happiness that You came to give me,

Quiet and at Rest

Rush rush, hurry hurry. Never enough time. Sound familiar?

You made a schedule that is too tight and too difficult, or someone else made your schedule too demanding. Stress, stress and more stress.

Sometimes the more efficient and successful you are, the more work is added to your agenda.

What to do? Is there a remedy?

Yes. And it centers in joy.

You may have heard that in the eye of a hurricane there is no wind. Tranquility reigns in that peaceful spot. Through Christ, you can find that place of peace in the midst of the storms that rage around you. Find it, and you become a calm observer of the storms rather than painfully enduring them.

I've long been plagued by the "hurry affliction."

It's something that our enemy uses to decrease our happiness and undermine our health. We, who suffer from this malady, may eat quickly to get on with other projects, and will make excuses to rush and scramble nearly all day long.

To this day I have to struggle to prevent this affliction from overriding the infinitely better way of living that God has taught me. Many mornings I awaken already tempted to hurry to get important "things" done. God has to help me or I slip back into my old ways of thinking. The principle the Holy Spirit has taught me that helps me the most is:

Merlin, you have only one thing to do today, and that is to please God.

We usually have plenty of excuses to be troubled and hurried, but Jesus still patiently waits for us to give our attention to infinitely more important things.

When I remember to think about pleasing God rather than finishing projects, the tenseness in my body and mind vanishes, and I begin to relax.

If you suffer from the hurry affliction, there is a cure. You will find it in believing that God is working good for you, in *whatever* you are doing. Washing dishes, scrubbing floors, cleaning up one mess after another, pounding nails, driving in traffic or whatever tasks are set before you, are opportunities to please Him. God is far more interested in what happens *in* us than in the tasks we complete. He gives His happiness to all those who dedicate their past, present and future to pleasing Him.

Our Potential

Throughout recorded history there have been people who excelled in their professions in ways that astonished those who understood their work. Scientists, doctors, politicians, military leaders, artists, and

Christian leaders have all said similar things about man's amazing potential. If people use their imagination, have big dreams, set goals, and really believe in something, they can surprise not only themselves, but everyone else too.

Jesus took men who were classified in their day as "ignorant and unlearned." He saw potential in them that they didn't see in themselves. Jesus also has more confidence in you and me than we have in ourselves – after all, He created us. He knows the unlimited potential that He has placed in each of us.

Jesus spent three years with twelve ordinary men and gave them extraordinary goals to reach. At the conclusion of their training time, the disciples had every reason to classify themselves as failures. They had blundered miserably, even at being a friend to Jesus. Jesus knew their deficiencies, but He believed in the power that God would give them. When they received that power, they had more influence on the world than any other twelve men in history.

Jesus told us we too could enjoy that same power from God, and that we too could accomplish anything if we believed in Him. Can we be filled with joy? Absolutely! He said we needed only to believe Him. Real joy doesn't come from things, people or accomplishments; neither is it withheld because of our lack of anything – except our lack of faith.

Plan to have new joy in Christ, today. Jesus described this joy in John 4:14: *The water I give him will become in him a spring of water welling up to eternal life.*

We should not concentrate on our own abilities, or lack thereof, because through Christ we can be whatever God calls us to be. The more we receive Christ's resources, the greater our joy will be!

Always remember what Paul says in 1 Corinthians

1:27-28: *God chose the foolish things of the world to shame the wise; God chose the weak things of the world to shame the strong. He chose the lowly things of this world and the despised things.*

Jesus centered His attention on people who were considered unlearned, powerless, and unsuccessful. He demonstrated His ability to use *anyone* to accomplish His plan, and He promised us great joy when we obey God by doing whatever He asks of us.

Not Our Home

This world is not our home. I often remind myself of this important fact. It helps me remember how unimportant my earthly problems really are.

There have been times when one day seemed to drag on forever. My days in Vietnam were often like that. Both the temperature and the humidity hovered at a sweltering 97 degrees. Death lurked all around us, and many men were angry and bitter. Each day in that deadly inferno seemed to last for weeks.

Now that I've been here on earth for 76 years, things seem different from the way I once perceived them. When I think back to my boyhood days, they seem to have been just . . . yesterday. Time sure has flown by. It's become obvious to me that: *Our days are like a fleeting shadow* (Ps. 144:4).

Our life on earth lasts but a moment of time in comparison to eternity. When I try to meditate on eternity, my mind soon flounders. How can I possibly comprehend that one day I will be in a place where I will live forever?

Jesus offers us the incredible opportunity to live in a place of perfection . . . forever! That's difficult to understand, but if we believe Him we should strive to comprehend what eternity means.

Sometimes we work for months to pay for a brief vacation. Jesus offers us far better terms. He said He will give us an *eternal* vacation! We serve Him for a brief time here on earth and He gives us *eternal joy*. That is the best bargain we will ever be offered!

What is Going On?

When I turned the water hose on, cold water burst all over me. I turned the water off and used two pairs of pliers to retighten the hose connection. This time the hose blew clear off the connection and water again went everywhere. Then I tried another hose. This one worked, but was too short. The third hose worked perfectly at the water faucet, but when I attached a spray at the other end it showered water in my face.

Something was definitely going on. I laid everything down and prayed for understanding of what I was supposed to learn. It always takes me a while to catch on!

The Holy Spirit whispered to my heart: You are frustrated and wishing you were not having all these problems with the water hose. You need to learn how to rejoice all the time.

Many of us long for, and dream of, opportunities to serve God in some "meaningful" way. A call to be a missionary, pastor, television evangelist, radio personality or youth leader, would spark an enthusiastic response. Opportunities to win people to Christ are high on our priority list.

God has only one you and one me. He is preparing us to fulfill His purposes. He wants to train us *now*. Seemingly unimportant, even bizarre incidents can be used by God to accomplish His plan. Frustrations, irritations, interruptions, setbacks, etc., are our opportunities to serve Him. We must declare and believe that such predicaments are God's will for us. He wants us to honor and praise Him *now*, in our present circumstances. If we accept frustrating situations as training opportunities, we *are* serving Him.

No ministry, no activity, no accomplishment is of greater importance to God than our honoring Him *now*! He is providing us the opportunities that He designed to fit our needs.

Even poverty can be a gift from God. Jesus saw a poor widow place two very small copper coins into a temple offering. He said, *I tell you the truth, this poor widow has put more into the treasury than all the others* (Mk. 12:43). She honored God as she gave Him all that she had, and Jesus honored her. Things that seem unimportant to us, may be all-important in God's eyes. God often takes the insignificant and uses it to give us *great joy* when we trust Him to do just that.

The Way God Created Us

Let's suppose that one hundred people eat a certain food, but only one person becomes ill – you. Why were the ninety-nine unaffected, yet you got sick? While we may never know the answer to that question, we do know one fact: you should not eat that particular food!

There are most likely some things in your life that irritate you, but have no unfavorable effect on other people. Although there may be no way to avoid those aggravating circumstances, there *are* ways to defeat them – you can force them to work *for* you.

First, we must recognize that whatever irritates us, steals our joy. The more irritating, the greater our loss of joy.

God created some of us with certain genes that allow particular foods to upset our digestive systems.

He also created some of us with the tendency to be irritated by things that other people may not even notice. That's God — always in the middle of everything, seeking our attention — always wanting us to understand that He is the Creator of everything.

We humans often rebel and whine, "God isn't fair. He allows things that make me unhappy." The question we must ask, though, is "*Why* does He allow things that He knows could make us unhappy?"

For openers, God uses all of life to help us realize that we carry rebellion and pride in our hearts. Weak, finite mortals that we are, we want to criticize God! We feel justified in thinking that God's creation is not as good as we could have produced. We see imperfections everywhere: in nature, animals, people, the past and present. Everything, in our opinion, needs to be changed.

The proud Saul met Jesus and became the humble Paul. He wrote, *Who are you to criticize God? Should the thing made say to the one who made it, "Why have you made me like this?"* (Ro. 9:20 (TLB).

The once angry Saul became a devout and happy man. His tormentors could beat, starve, stone, and imprison him — things that would highly "irritate" the average person. But not Paul. He saw *everything* as an instrument of God to bring him joy.

We may cry out to God and beg Him to change the things that irritate us. Not so with Paul. His love for and faith in God had progressed beyond such reactions. Paul believed that God was blessing him in and through *everything*. Paul lived on a level of commitment far above the average person. He understood that the trials and imperfections of this world are the perfect conditions in which to receive the joys that Christ came to bring us.

We too can look these irritations in the face and

say, "Although Satan would love for you to steal my joy, I believe you are being used by God to do what needs to be done in me."

No Longer Troubled

Being worried or upset can quickly deplete our happiness.

It was a glorious day for Martha. Jesus, the Messiah her people had longed for, was headed toward her village. She may have said to her sister, "Mary, wouldn't it be wonderful if we could get Jesus to come and eat with us?" Then it happened – He came. I imagine this was the most exciting day of her life. She probably launched into a frenzy of activity to get her best recipes prepared. She would want everything in perfect order.

Then He arrived. She undoubtedly greeted Him with enthusiasm and delight. This was to be a very happy day.

Then something happened that took the glow from Martha's heart. Her sister, Mary, didn't cooperate. Instead of helping, she went into the living room, sat down and contentedly listened to Jesus. Dinner would never be ready on time without Mary's help. In Martha's mind, it must have been essential that Jesus not be kept waiting.

Martha probably made numerous hand signals to Mary, urging her to come and help get dinner ready for the most special man in the whole world. But Mary didn't budge.

In exasperation, Martha finally went to Jesus, hoping to get His understanding and help. She said, *Lord, don't you care that my sister has left me to do the work by myself? Tell her to help me* (Lu. 10:40).

How frequently you and I have approached God

with an attitude similar to Martha's, "God, I'm upset, but You know I have a good reason!" We are usually quite certain that our reasons for being irritated are fully justified.

If it had been me, I probably would have encouraged Mary to go help her sister. But Jesus was more interested in *helping* Martha than in hearing her complaints. *Martha, Martha*, the Lord answered, *you are worried and upset about many things* (Lu. 10:41).

That moment may have been the most transforming incident of Martha's life. Jesus' words caused her to realize the kind of person she had become — worried, troubled, upset about many things.

Later on it was evident that Martha had changed. Lazarus became seriously ill and the two sisters sent word to Jesus. When Martha heard that Jesus was coming, she *quickly* went out to meet Him.

It seems clear that Martha felt no resentment over the words Jesus had spoken to her. Some of us would. We would not be pleased if we told someone what was bothering us, and they responded with,

"You worry a lot, don't you."

But instead of retreating in indignation, Martha accepted Jesus' words. John 11:5 describes Jesus' special feelings toward her: *Jesus loved Martha and her sister and Lazarus.*

When Lazarus died, Martha made a declaration to Jesus that described her faith. She said to Him: *God will give you whatever you ask* (Jn. 11:22).

We too can trust that if Jesus wants to do something for us, He will do it! We too can say to Him. *God will give you whatever you ask.*

Later Jesus performed a miracle for Martha: *Jesus called in a loud voice, Lazarus, come out!* (Jn. 11:43).

I remember when Jesus revealed to me, *Merlin, Merlin, you are worried and upset about many things.*

I understood what He meant. Fortunately I paid close attention, and soon began to experience wonderful changes in my attitude about *many things*. Today, I'm still worried and upset about some things, but I promise you that it happens on far fewer occasions. Like Martha, I have learned that it really pays to listen to what Jesus says.

This could be an important moment for you, too, if like Martha you have been troubled about many things. I believe also that God will give us new answers to our prayers, and great joy as we learn not to be troubled.

Irritations That Lift Us

We all have opportunities to be irritated about something. Each irritation that we accept adds yet another burden to our already overtaxed minds and emotions. By the end of the day we can be physically and emotionally exhausted. Unless . . . we learn how to deal with those people and things that interrupt what *we* want our days to be like.

Each event we experience has its own potential either to *lift* us or *discourage* us. When our teenagers ignore our advice; when our parents ignore what we try to explain; when our employees take all the pay they can get, but do as little work as possible; when you work with all your heart, but your boss only expects more; when your back aches, but you never get your work done. At the very least, these things change us in some way.

How do we find joy and peace in the midst of all these irritants?

When I was young I envied older people. They didn't have to strive to get an education or establish a career. They never had to put up with all the hassles that plague young people. But then I became one of the "older generation." Since then I've learned that the older you get, the more irritations you become subjected to. As the body tires, more and more things become potential drainers of energy and joy. But because we're God's children, we can learn to compel irritations to *lift* us rather than discourage us.

Irritations can drain happiness out of anyone. But as we resist temptations to be angry or frustrated, each incident then creates good in us! As we learn to cast off the yoke of irritation, we gain new freedom. Joy takes on new meaning as we learn to let The Creator *create happiness* in us. This is one reason Jesus came to earth – that His joy could be in us (see Jn. 15:11). Jesus takes what is frustrating and uses it to create happiness. A miracle? Yes, but no more so than His raising Lazarus from the dead.

The Key to . . . Everything

The San Diego Chargers football team was playing on their own turf, and they were losing in a big way. The local fans were groaning, even booing. But mixed with this, some fans were cheering. Others looked at them as if they were traitors – how could they be cheering when their team was losing?

But some observers paid closer attention. Those cheering had radios that were tuned in to the San Diego Padre's World Series baseball game, and the Padres were winning! That was what made these local fans cheer! But those who had no radios didn't know the good news.

Some Christians are "tuned in" to God's Word, the Good News that tells them God is working for their good (see Ro. 8:28). They rejoice because they believe He is keeping His promise to them. Other people can see only the unhappy things going on around them, so they don't have a clue why some Christians are so happy.

If you are not one of the happy Christians, you may not be tuned in to the miracles that are going on around you.

If the sky is a beautiful blue, what good does it do us if we don't even notice it? If a flock of birds are singing a happy song, what good does such joyous music do us if we don't pay attention to the symphony?

Our happiness nearly always depends on what we pay attention to. There are many reasons to be joyful, but if we see and dwell upon only unhappy things, we will not recognize the good that God provides us.

So let's begin to focus more attention on the good things. Let's rejoice if our feet are pain free, if our eyes can see, our ears hear, our knees and necks will bend. If we have someone to love, work to do, a church to attend, songs to sing or music to hear, we need to pay attention to them. If there are sunsets to watch, food to eat, clothing and shoes to wear – our joy will still depend on what we *pay attention to*.

We can begin a new way of life that will cause God to open the windows of Heaven and give us more happiness than we have ever dreamed possible.

Pick out something for which you are especially thankful. If it is your feet, take a walk and concentrate on them. With every step thank God for feet that will carry you. Sing a song about your feet, and rejoice that they take you where you want to go. Tomorrow, revel in what you can see, or hear. The next day, rejoice in the people you can love.

Keep being thankful. Let thankfulness become a way of life. Your spirit will rejoice in what God is doing. Your happiness depends on what you pay attention to. It really does. Giving thanks to God is the key to . . . *everything*.

Faith That is Unnatural

Abraham was an old man with no children, but he accepted God's challenge to believe that one day he would become the father of a great nation. There was *no evidence* that God's promise would ever be fulfilled.

Years later there were over a million people in Abraham's family, but they were slaves. God challenged Moses to believe that He would lead them to their Promised Land. Again, there was no evidence that it would ever happen.

God has called you and me to trust Him regarding many situations, including the well-being of our families. Like Abraham and Moses, we too can decide to trust Him. Or, we can fail to believe.

When we agonize over problems involving our families or friends, we may feel as if we are only doing what is right and natural. Faith, however, is usually quite *unnatural*. Faith requires that we base our joy and peace of mind on things we do not see, feel, or even comprehend.

Abraham and other Old Testament heroes had the same emotions as you and I. They, too would have loved to see more confirmation that God was going to help them. But they had to believe God's promises, just as you and I do.

God places us in circumstances that He designs uniquely for us, just as surely as He designed events for Abraham and Moses. Our tasks and responsibilities are not the same as theirs, but we have the same spiritual choices to make. We can live in fear and anxiety, and allow those painful emotions to control our hearts,or we can choose to believe that God will honor our trust in Him.

Now is the perfect time to rejoice in what you believe He is doing!

A Perfect Plan

I had heard about you before, but now I have seen you (Job 42:5 TLB). Before Job lost his possessions, his children, and his health, he had heard about God, but had not "seen" Him. Job did not understand why such terrible afflictions had come upon him, or why he seemed to be forsaken by God. His friends urged him to stop sinning, and repent, so that God would give him good instead of bad things.

But Job had a problem. He couldn't ask God to forgive him, because he didn't know what he had done wrong. And even God said He didn't find anything wrong in Job! These multiple tragedies caused Job to question God's fairness. But God eventually convinced Job that he was foolish to doubt His plan.

You and I may wonder why we have to endure life's difficult trials, but our trials are nothing compared to Job's. Unlike Job, we know about our past and present sins, sins that God could use to condemn us if He so desired. Yet we still question His goodness when bad things happen.

We need to see God as He *is,* and as Job eventually saw Him. Having seen Him, Job said that even if he knew God was going to kill him, he would still trust Him (see Job 13:15).

When Things Go Wrong

Jonah didn't want to go where God had told him – Nineveh. He was on his way elsewhere, to another city. But now the ship was sinking. Jonah had *gone down into the lowest parts of the ship, had lain down, and was fast asleep* (Jonah 1:5 NKJ). Although he was disobeying God, he was at peace while the ship's crew struggled to save their lives. It's not unusual for us to be indifferent when we too are disobeying God. *The captain came to him, and said to him,"What do you mean, sleeper? Arise, call on your God"* (Vs. 6).

We may need someone to say, "Yes, you act happy sometimes, but when things happen that you don't like you are miserable to be around." The true test of our happiness is when we *don't* get what we want. Then we may not be the at-peace-people we think we are. Our happiness may depend on things being pleasant, comfortable, enjoyable and agreeable with our desires.

Jonah had a lesson to learn, and the sailors were willing to teach him. Better for him to be thrown overboard and drowned than them!

When people reveal some flaw in us, we may be inclined to "throw them overboard". Who are they to insinuate that we are wrong? And if God wants us to change, *He* can tell us!

But God uses people and circumstances to reveal our weaknesses. They are His servants to accomplish His purposes. He uses good people, bad people, saints and sinners. And He often uses whoever will be the most distasteful to us. We can remain unhappy until we finally learn what He wants to teach us.

You and I are on our way to our "Nineveh" (the place we don't want to go). One way or another, we will arrive. God calls us to go joyfully. That may not be easy for us, since we are rebellious children. But we can stop grumbling, and decide to go wherever God wants to take us. By the time we arrive, we will have learned *how to be happy*!

Our Year of Jubilee

God gave the Jews a special law regarding the year of Jubilee, which came every fifty years. At that time all land would return to its original owners, all slaves set free, and all bills marked paid in full. This was the law of the land.

Imagine how excited people would be as that year approached. What celebrating there must have been as families were reunited.

The law required each person to make a clear claim to his own property or freedom. When his freedom was received, he was then free once again to sell himself into slavery. I doubt, however, that many sold themselves into bondage again.

Jesus said you and I were once slaves: *I tell you the truth, everyone who sins is a slave to sin* (Jn. 8:34). Christ made it possible for us to receive our freedom, but we too must claim that freedom: *It is for freedom that Christ has set us free. Stand firm, then, and do not let yourselves be burdened again by a yoke of slavery* (Ga. 5:1).

When we are under Satan's control, everything and everyone has the ability to make us unhappy. Everything! Family, friends, job, money, health, or the environment – any of these things can control how we feel.

But when we claim the freedom that Christ has given us, other people cannot control our happiness. Jesus didn't come into the world so that we would remain under bondage. He proved that He is able to free us from the slavery of unhappiness.

If you are being oppressed by unhappiness, claim your freedom. Be rescued from whatever has deprived you of your priceless right to be free. Act now, and this can be *your* year of Jubilee!

Offensive People

A man sent me a letter that was perhaps the most challenging I had ever received. It was filled with accusations about the evil things he believed I had done.

My natural inclination was to ask him to submit some evidence to substantiate his absurd allegations, and to quote scriptures to him about his judging others. I even thought about sending him a list of people who could defend my character.

However, it didn't take long before the Holy Spirit convicted me. God was not interested in what I thought about the man's denunciations. He wanted me to see what was going on in my *own* heart. Soon I realized that I, too, had jumped on the bandwagon of judging others.

When I asked God to bless and encourage the letter writer, my frustrations faded away. The following day I received a FAX from the man in which he asked me to forgive him for the "terrible things" he had written. He explained that his wife was in the hospital with an incurable disease, the hospital was insisting that he take her home to die, and his heart was filled with bitterness toward God and everyone on earth. As I read his FAX, I realized how terrible it would have been for me to respond to him with the same spirit that he had displayed.

When a clerk, waitress or anyone else treats you with impolite words or attitudes, how do you feel like responding? Do you feel like giving them a piece of your mind? When we have such experiences we need to, for our own benefit, ask God to bless and help that person.

People who act rudely or unfriendly toward us, nearly always need us to respond as Jesus would. They may have received word that their spouse wants a divorce, their child has an incurable disease, a parent is dying, or that they are going to be fired. The list of what might be happening to them is nearly endless. If you or I were in their shoes, we might be unable to work because of our grief.

Of course, some people act disagreeable *every day*, but the question is, why are they that way? We don't have to approve of the way they act, or reward them for their rudeness, but we can learn how to cause that person's unpleasantness to create joy in us. Is that possible? Yes it is. And the more we learn to do this, the more in tune we become with the Holy Spirit, and the more our happiness will increase!

Learning Secrets

You can learn the secrets of joy.

Everyone wants, and everyone looks for, joy. We can find it in full stomachs, vacations, work that we enjoy, friends, spouses and children.

The problem is that stomachs don't stay full, vacations end, work becomes tedious, friends sometimes leave, marriage problems come, and children grow up. When happy things end, what happens then? Too often sadness sets in.

Have you considered the possibility that many things that *seem* to produce joy may eventually rob us of what we *really* want?

If you have been seeking joy in *things* that fade away with time, why not consider a new source? The Apostle Paul did, and he was highly successful. When painful things came to him, he learned how to turn them into joy. Now *that's* a wonderful goal for all of us!

Paul kept urging us to try his solutions. He had no criticism for finding joy in traditional, legitimate ways, but he demonstrated that joy can be found in *everything* that happens to us. Paul would not be such a credible witness if he himself had not suffered in so many ways. Most of his friends deserted him – even those he had helped to receive eternal life. His church and government plotted to kill him. He was hungry, beaten, and stoned. He had little ability as an orator and, we're told, was not even pleasing in appearance.

Yet Paul saw himself as a man filled with joy in all his trials. He demonstrated that nothing and no one could prevent him from entering into the joy that he had received from God.

My own journey toward spiritual joy has been exciting. I once was a miserably unhappy person because I thought life had been unfair to me. Now I see that joy is like a secret gold mine waiting to be discovered. Once we understand and follow God's instructions, life takes on an entirely new meaning. We can shout to God with triumph, for we see that in His perfect wisdom He has surrounded us with unlimited opportunities to experience His joy.

Laughter Can Fade

Some people know how to make us laugh. Movie directors use their skills to arouse our laughter. Writers and actors can create plots that produce nearly irresistible humor.

But laughter can quickly fade, leaving the amused observers to slide back into empty, dull unhappiness.

The joy that God wants to shine into our hearts has a life expectancy of . . . eternity. We may not always enjoy the same intense feelings, but joy is always there waiting to administer healing to the wounds we receive during our journey here on earth.

Joy is like a secret ointment that heals our emotions. God offers us His remedy – a way to live in a sin-corrupted environment, yet not feel miserable.

Sometimes we look for miraculous, new solutions to problems rather than receive what God has already provided for us. An unhappy Christian may demand that specific problems be solved before he will be happy. If so, he is striving to reverse God's intended order. A happy faith in God needs to come *first*. Then, as our faith grows, it causes our joy to grow. And increased joy produces even more faith. Faith and joy work together to help us trust in God rather than insisting on His miracles.

People sometimes approached Jesus with wrong, selfish motives. You and I may also come to Him with selfish motives: *And even when you do ask you don't get it because your whole aim is wrong – you want only what will give you pleasure* (Ja. 4:3 TLB).

God has His own plan, and that plan is to prepare us for eternity.

Spiritual joy is the very best remedy for any problem we will ever encounter. We can say, "God is in charge of His children, and I am His child. I receive every blessing He wants to give me, and I accept His decisions as being perfect." Do this with the assurance that God is working for your good.

God's Score Cards

There are many "impossible things" being done by ordinary people like you and me. God has called us to achieve results that unbelievers consider impossible.

Paul learned to delight in the most incredible things. In 2 Corinthians 12:10, he says he delighted in weakness, insults, hardships, persecutions and difficulties. He also discovered that the less strength he had, the more he depended on God.

That point of view is puzzling to some of us. I don't believe God is displeased if we fail to duplicate Paul's victories, but I believe He is displeased if we refuse to even *try* to reach that goal. God paid too high a price when He permitted His Son to suffer; too high for us simply to shrug our shoulders and profess lack of understanding.

God wants us to try to learn to be delighted in *everything*. He offers all that He is to help us. He accepts our mistakes, our failures and our weaknesses, but He does not accept our *unwillingness to try*.

Remember the parable of the talents? One man hid his because he was afraid he couldn't use it properly. He tried to excuse himself, but the master had him cast into prison. The other men in the illustration were richly rewarded because they used to the best of their ability what their master had given them.

God has given you the potential to rejoice in Him ALWAYS. What a grand possibility! Some of us find it quite easy to rejoice most of the time. Others of us may find it difficult to rejoice even part of the time. Regardless of how little faith we may have, if we decide to do nothing toward reaching God's goals for us, we may be in big trouble.

Rejoice as much and as often as you are capable of doing. As you do, God will encourage your spirit, and you will discover your ability to *rejoice even more*.

Illogical

If we expect God to work good for us in a "logical" manner, we may be disappointed, because He often works in ways that seem illogical to us.

God did not follow human logic when He chose an unmarried girl to be the mother of the Savior of the world. He could have waited until the eve of Mary's wedding before He caused her to become pregnant. That way, she and Joseph and their families would have been spared a lifetime of embarrassment. Mary probably had to stretch her faith in order to believe that God would work good in her seemingly impossible situation.

Noah could have said, "God, if you want me to work on this ark, why don't You have me build it in a logical place – near some water?"

Many of the people God uses in special ways could say, "This isn't logical, God. Why are You doing it this way?"

God's ways are as mysterious as the pathway of the wind (Ec. 11:5 TLB).

You and I can spend our time endlessly questioning God – Why this? Why that? Or we can look at every situation in our lives and joyfully expect God to work something good for us. He may or may not provide what we consider a logical solution, but we should believe that He is always interested in our welfare. James 1:2 doesn't seem at all logical, yet it is nevertheless a key to joy: *Consider it pure joy, my brothers, whenever you face trials of many kinds*.

Verse three is also not pleasant to our ears: *The testing of your faith develops perseverance*. Our human nature prefers to get things accomplished without any trials or uncertainty being involved.

Remember when your teachers insisted that you persevere in school and gradually you learned to read? God, too, wants us to persevere, because He knows the indescribable joys He has planned for us.

A Happy Revelation

The following information can solve a dilemma that you may have had since you first became a Christian: How to love God with all your heart while also loving other people as much as you love yourself. Jesus considered these our two most important goals.

If we love God, and other people, we should be a blessing to them both. Has anyone ever told you how you could be a blessing to both by doing only *one* thing? Wouldn't it be great if you could be a blessing to God *and* other folks, and at the same time enjoy it more than you have ever enjoyed anything?

The secret is in learning how to receive the special joy that God wants to give us. Contrary to popular opinion, God wants His children to have an abundance of His joy. Our cheerful delight will help others find God's happiness as we tell them the *source* of our joy.

When we were youngsters if another child told us we were ugly or dumb, those thoughts could become imbedded in our minds. We could decide that we were indeed unattractive or unintelligent. Those unhappy thoughts could stay with us all of our lives!

For thoughts to be most effective, they must be frequently repeated in our minds. If we dwell upon a certain thought long enough, we will eventually accept it as a *fact*. If thinking what is *not* true about ourselves can have such a strong influence over us, think how much we could be changed if we frequently repeat thoughts about ourselves that *are* true.

If we truly believe that Jesus is our Savior, the more we think of Him as our Savior the more real and powerful that thought becomes. Such inspired thoughts then have incredible power in us. We can learn to think other inspiring thoughts too, thoughts that lift us into becoming increasingly happy and therefore more pleasing to God and more helpful to others.

We have many opportunities each day to think thoughts that will help us to become increasingly happy people. I am so loved by God that He will cause everything I see, hear, know, remember, or encounter to bring increasing happiness to my heart and to the hearts of all my loved ones. We should repeat these thoughts constantly until, by God's grace, they change us.

As you persist in thinking happy, uplifting thoughts, you will soon be delighted at how powerful and effective God has made them.

Destroying Happiness

Ecclesiastes 6:2 tells us that a man could have wealth, job satisfaction, and be honored by others, but still be unhappy. If we want to be happy, it is important to understand that *we must obey God!*

Jesus gave men one very clear injunction. He said: *Anyone who looks at a woman lustfully has already committed adultery with her in his heart* (Mt. 5:28). If we allow our minds to dwell on immoral thoughts, we stimulate ever-increasing desires that will attack the very core of our happiness. To emphasize this point, write a list of the potential unhappy results of immorality. You might be surprised at how lengthy your list could be. Remember that immoral thoughts are actively sowing seeds of destruction in the heart! These seeds may take time to grow and mature, but they will eventually develop into destructive actions. James 1:15 (TLB) gives us a clear warning: *Evil thoughts lead to evil actions and afterwards to the death penalty from God.* James addressed that admonition to his "dear brothers."

Christians can ignore what Jesus said and blissfully continue immoral thinking – wrongly assuming that such thoughts are beyond our control. But 2 Corinthians 10:5 assures us that we can *take captive every thought to make it obedient to Christ.* For years I wrestled with what seemed to be an unbeatable enemy. When I had an impure thought I felt acutely guilty. Then I would determine to never again let my thoughts be disobedient to Christ. But at a moment when I least expected it, impure thoughts would flash through my mind. I was sure there had to be a way to defeat the devices of the enemy, so I kept telling God that I knew He could lead me into victory. And He taught me what to do! Now, when I see, or think of, an attractive woman, or look at her picture, I concentrate on thinking the following:

God designed her.

He created her.

She belongs to Him.

By the time I've meditated on these three truths, I'm delivered from having thoughts that would displease God. When our thoughts are "obedient to Christ," His Spirit works wonderful things in us. Instead of our disobedience *preventing* us from being happy, our effort to obey *causes* us to be happy! Consider this happy thought: *God keeps him occupied with gladness of heart* (Ec. 5:20).

(Ladies, please urge the men and boys in your life to read the above section).

Happy Thought Patterns

Have you ever wondered why your mind sometimes keeps replaying unhappy thoughts? You keep thinking about people who have mistreated you, family problems, physical ailments, unpaid bills, etc. You wish you could turn these negative thoughts off, but it seems you can't.

Some folks become ensnared in the "Grouchy Thought Syndrome," and before they know it they are perpetual grouches. In most situations their minds click in with, "This is something to be grouchy about." Eventually even their faces reflect their unhappy thoughts. People who encounter them see a grouch.

Other people worry excessively. They become so steeped in worry that they see something in nearly every circumstance that requires even more worry. Before they realize it, they are continually worried about something.

Thoughts can be compared to a path through a field. Each time that path is trodden, it becomes easier to follow. Thoughts create similar paths through our minds that, in time, become increasingly easy to follow. The mind gets into a groove, or way of thinking, and eventually that groove becomes a habit. Even if the person wants to get rid of that thought pattern, the mind doggedly churns away at its destructive behavior.

The mind does the work it was created to do – it *thinks.* And when it thinks worrisome thoughts, it causes anxiety and fear.

But we *can* reprogram harmful thought patterns. That's why the Bible teaches us to "rejoice always." When we follow that command, the brain learns to do what? To rejoice always!

Paul's thoughts were dominated by his hatred of Christians, but when he met and accepted Jesus, his thoughts changed. They changed so much that even when he was chained in prison, hungry, cold or beaten, he rejoiced. His triumph in Christ was so great that his mind could only repeat, *Joy, joy, joy.*

Joy. What a wonderful emotion to have in control

of our thoughts. The more we dwell upon and repeat these "joy-thoughts," the happier we become.

Our Authority

When I was a Private in the U.S. Army, I had no authority over anyone. I could not compel anyone to do anything. But the moment I became a commissioned officer, many new advantages were available to me. Little did I realize as a young Lieutenant how many more advantages I would have when I eventually became a Lieutenant Colonel.

Before we become children of God, we have no idea of the advantages we will gain. At the moment Jesus becomes our Savior, all the authority that God offers His children becomes ours! We may not know what those benefits are, but they are ours just the same. In time, and through persistence, we can learn much more about the blessings that are ours in Christ.

One advantage of our new status is the victory that Jesus promised us. Jesus provided us the authority to be victorious over . . . everything. *Everyone born of God overcomes the world. This is the victory that has overcome the world, even our faith* (1 Jn. 5:4).

If you are unhappy about troublesome circumstances in your life, you may still be dragging along with the same paltry benefits as an Army Private. If so, consider the abundant joy that Jesus came to give us. He taught us that we could enjoy the benefit of trusting God to supply everything we need. We would be foolish to depend on ourselves, when God wants to place us under *His* protection. In ourselves, we have about as much authority over life's problems as a Private has over an Officer. But in Christ we have the authority to compel our problems to work *for* us rather than against us (see Rom. 8:28). That is *good* news! The more we understand and claim that benefit, the greater our joy becomes.

Before I realized the authority I had over my difficulties, I did what came naturally. I worried. I grumbled. I complained. But when I understood the authority that God has given us, I started telling my problems, "God will *make* you work for my good." What an eye-opening revelation that was, and what delightful blessings I have received as a result!

I urge you to enjoy the authority God has given you!

Going "All the Way"

We came for many different reasons and from assorted backgrounds, into the ranks of those brash young men known as *Paratroopers*. How proud of ourselves we were!

It wasn't that way in the beginning. Most of us had never been near an airplane. Jumping *out* of one seemed daring, exciting and adventurous – but scary. Later we learned that our brand of adventure was dangerous – really dangerous. But our instructors inspired us to subdue our fear and jump out of airplanes while high above the ground – to *want* to do it! How did they manage that? They taught us to believe in ourselves.

They convinced us that we were the best men in the entire armed forces. The very best in the world. That was no easy task, but they found ways to persuade us.

During all parts of our training we were reminded repeatedly that airborne troops were the best of the best. Whenever an enlisted man approached an officer, he would shout, "All the way, sir!" The officer would proudly respond, "Airborne!" We repeated those words many times every day. We prided ourselves in being willing to go "all the way." That meant anytime, anywhere.

To be ready and eager for action, we young men needed to believe that we were fully able to do *anything*. Were we? No, but we believed we were. Our training had convinced us that we were invincible, so we approached each mission with complete confidence.

Our mission as Christians also requires that we have complete confidence in all situations. Experience, however, has taught us that undo confidence in *ourselves* is always doomed to disappointment and failure. These failures, in turn, make us feel defeated and discouraged. We need to be trained to place our confidence where it belongs – in Christ. I often repeat to myself, "I have the righteousness of Christ."

That simple truth is not easy to grasp, so I repeat it until my faith and joy come alive. I, Merlin, actually have the righteousness of Christ! I have it because I have accepted this wonderful gift *that comes from God*. The more I declare and meditate on this miracle, the greater my happiness becomes and my confidence in Christ increases. The reality of what God has done for us is beyond my power to grasp with my intellect, but it creates great joy within me.

If you have not believed in and enjoyed this miracle, now is the time to go "all the way" with God, and accept the gift of happiness that He offers you.

What We Concentrate On

You will keep in perfect peace him whose mind is steadfast, because he trusts in you (Is. 26:3). Have you ever read a book while you were ill, that was so interesting it took your mind completely off your pain?

For as long as the book steadfastly held your attention, you could forget your hurting body.

A soldier in battle can have a severe wound yet keep moving forward if his mind is so fixed (steadfast) on his mission that he ignores his injury.

The reverse is also true. We can concentrate so intensely on a problem that it becomes the only thing we think about. Luke 21:34 says, *Be careful, or your hearts will be weighed down with . . . the anxieties of life*. If we concentrate on our problems we can actually become incapable of handling other important matters. Being weighed down with the anxieties of life shows that we lack faith in God.

When I was flying my Mooney 201 airplane, my attention was on my instruments nearly all the time. I had been trained to scan the many dials from left to right, so I would always know what the engine was doing. Every few minutes I checked the fuel, manifold pressure, propeller revolutions per minute, oil pressure, temperature readings, altitude, air speed and other instruments that reported how the plane was running.

The engine overcame the continual downward pull of gravity, but I never concentrated on gravity: my focus was always on the engine that was holding me up.

If a pilot concentrates on the ground, do you know where he will end up? That's right, on the ground. Driving a car is the same. If we look too long to the right or left, we will find ourselves drifting in that direction.

Problems are always trying to pull us in the wrong direction – all we need to do is concentrate on them. The natural mind *always* wants to dwell on problems. You probably have experienced this many times yourself. Just as it takes power to keep an airplane flying, it requires considerable force to keep our minds away from our troubles.

Mary and I live beside a beautiful lake. It is a delight to relax in a lawn chair and watch the panorama of nature. Swans, ducks and other waterfowl parade by our home. As the sun marches overhead, the shadows form ever-changing patterns.

One day while enjoying our view, I suddenly thought about the life and death struggle that goes on in the animal kingdom. I began to study what lay before me from a different point of view.

The birds in the air were seeking one thing – fish. When they spotted one, they dove, and the fish lived no more.

Beneath the water another battle raged. One fish devours a smaller one. Then a larger fish attacks the victor. On and on the struggle continues.

What appears to be a peaceful scene is actually a desperate battle that never ends. If I should concentrate on the life and death struggle being fought in our lake, I could never enjoy its beauty. My mind would always drift back to other wars in which I saw men fight and die. So I concentrate on the beauty that surrounds our peaceful lake.

What we concentrate on nearly always determines whether we *enjoy* life or merely *endure* it. We can see good things, or we can focus our attention on pain and evil. The choice is ours. God doesn't ask us to deny the existence of suffering; rather, He asks us to look beyond the pain of this world so we can see His perfect plan for us.

If we spend our lives focusing on our problems or on those of the people around us, we will never see what *God is doing*. When we concentrate on God's relationship with His people, we realize that He is our Problem Solver and our Peace.

Interfering in God's Business

People can be frustrating. Or have you already noticed? You can be having a day in which everything is going great and you are bubbling over with joy. Then along comes that person who frustrates or angers you. What do you do then?

Recently a close associate did something that I knew was wrong. Before I confronted him I prayed for wisdom. But the more I prayed the more confusing the issue became. If I were going to help this person I needed to confront him in a way that would help rather than harm. However I presented the problem, though, I believed he would be upset and probably resent whatever I had to say on the subject. On the other hand, I felt I needed to say or do something – but what?

The more I prayed, the more baffled I became. Praying usually gives me joy, but not this time. What was happening?   I was learning! I was learning something that could help you should you ever face a similar situation.

The Lord spoke to my spirit, and repeated what He told Peter: *What is that to you? You follow me* (Jn. 21:22 TLB).

"Yes, Lord, but what should I do about this person?"

You have only one concern. Do what will please Me.

"Yes, Lord, I know that is what I must do, but what will please You?"

You are not at peace while you are thinking about that person. Turn him over to Me.

The moment I listened to God, my peace returned.

Other people belong to God, not to us! About ninety-nine percent of the time it is God's business to correct others, not ours. If we are a parent, supervisor or pastor, we are sometimes obligated to make decisions to correct someone. But most of us are seldom in a position where we have the responsibility to correct "His servants." When we feel compelled to do what is God's business, we will nearly always feel frustrated, and lose our joy. How delightful it is when we learn to trust God to run His business of conforming others to the image of Christ . . . without our help!

Receiving Perfection

Do your imperfections sometimes make you feel miserable?

I once belonged to a church that placed great emphasis on Christian perfection. For years I suffered over the many flaws I saw in myself. I meditated on scriptures such as Matthew 5:48: *Be perfect, therefore, as your heavenly Father is perfect.*

I saw perfection as the only status in which I could ever hope to be really happy. Until that day arrived, I would labor diligently until I became more pleasing to God. After years of frustration, I finally came to understand that Jesus had given us an objective that could never be reached by our *own* efforts. Perfection is achieved only by receiving Christ's perfection as His gift. Understanding that has produced great joy within me.

Jesus came to do for us what we cannot do for ourselves. We aren't even able to comprehend what real perfection is. However, our imperfections can become stepping-stones to greater dependence upon Christ.

Many Christians languish in the quagmire of their

defeats. They have failed to receive the blessings that Jesus intended for them. Because of Jesus, however, our sadness can be turned into joy, and our lives infused with increasing happiness as we fix our attention on what He desires to accomplish in us.

Know the Source!

Jesus told His disciples that He was going to Jerusalem where He would be killed and in three days be resurrected. Satan whispered to Peter, "No, He should not do that," so Peter told Jesus what was on his mind. But Jesus understood that Satan was trying to tempt Him into disobeying God. Jesus turned and said to Peter, *Get behind me, Satan!* (Mt. 16:23).

What if one of the other disciples had told Peter that Satan was giving him wrong thoughts? Peter may have argued, and replied, "No, my thoughts are right. I'm trying to keep Jesus from being killed."

One of the best ways for us to increase our happiness is to know when Satan is tempting us to disobey God.

For example, the Bible makes it clear that God forbids us to think immoral thoughts. Just as Satan caused Peter to think wrong thoughts, he tries to cause immoral thoughts and desires within us. Once we understand the *source* of such thoughts, we can then *resist the devil* (Ja. 4:7).

When forbidden thoughts tempt us, we can know that they are from Satan, our enemy. And when we understand that Satan can give us thoughts that displease God, we can stop believing that we just can't help ourselves. We can replace those thoughts with thoughts of God's mighty power to help us. We can think how good God is to us. How great His mercy is to send Jesus to purchase us with His precious blood.

It is crucial that we learn to do this, because Satan delights in using his power of suggestion to lead unwary people into great unhappiness.

Just before a man is about to think an immoral thought, Satan will often urge him to focus on a woman's body. In the same way, Satan urged Eve to focus her attention on the forbidden fruit. When she did, she *saw that the fruit of the tree was good for food and pleasing to the eye* (Ge. 3:6).

And the rest is history.

When Satan tries to tempt us into self-pity, we might hear, "You aren't being treated fairly. You have a good reason to be unhappy." But God, Who wants us to be happy, will help us resist Satan's temptations.

Since God has given each of us different personalities, something that tempts me to be selfish, worried or irritable may not tempt you. Therefore, evil spirits will devise tactics that are best suited to appeal to and attack our individual weakness. Satan used such a tactic against Peter, who was prone to act first and think later.

The more we resist Satan's strategy to give us thoughts that displease God, the happier we will be!

Because of Christ's victory over Satan, we too are victorious, and can do whatever God commands us. So rejoice! Rejoice in the triumph that Christ has given you!

Every Breath

If you have a problem, you need to read this chapter. If you have many problems, you *very much* need to read it. If you have *no* problems, you still need to read it.

Remember the feelings you had when you looked forward to a birthday party, Christmas, the last day of school, a vacation or, a date with the heartthrob of your dreams? The anticipation you felt may have been as enjoyable as the events themselves. Expecting happy things triggers emotions that are difficult to describe; yet we know those feelings are real.

So we know that happy events don't actually have to happen before we can experience joy. Just our *confidence* that something we want is going to happen, can cause us joy.

Our confidence that God will eventually do something good for us, causes joy – NOW. The more good we expect, the greater our happiness becomes.

I first learned to believe that God would cause *small problems* to work for my good. Then I learned to believe that He would use more difficult problems to work even greater good for me. In time I began to enjoy my assurance in Him even *before* He solved a problem. My belief that God would work every problem for my good created an ever-increasing confidence within me. The more my confidence grew, the greater my happiness became.

But then came the monotonous, uninteresting times when nothing new or unusual seemed to be happening. Everyday, commonplace events often seemed empty of any opportunity for God to work anything for my good. This presented me with a new challenge: To learn to believe that God can cause ordinary, and even dull times to work for our good.

This was a difficult, but highly rewarding adventure for me. God taught me that He is *always* is working for our good, and that even ordinary times and situations have their value if we have faith. Our faith should be strong *all* the time, not just during times of trouble or crisis.

Our lives can be likened to a motion picture film containing a large number of single pictures. When these individual pictures of our lives are connected, they become a unified "moving picture". This moving picture runs its course until finally it comes to "The End."

This movie reel is held together by each picture, or frame. If the film were to be cut, the frames would unsplice, and the projector could not operate the movie until repairs were made.

Our moments here on earth were choreographed by God, our Savior Director, to progress step-by-step (picture-by-picture) toward their final end -our destiny in eternity.

When I'm frustrated by some person or event, I sometimes think of my life as resembling a continuing film that is moving toward its end. Each event of my life, each frame, is necessary if my life – my "movie" – is to reach its ultimate conclusion. This analogy is helpful to me as I experience the trials and stresses of life.

Once we see each event of our lives as part of God's plan for us, we realize that every episode is important, and creates great joy is us.

More Pleasing to God

We must all appear before the judgment seat of Christ . . . (2 Co. 5:10). Our prayers could prevent us from being as happy as God wants us to be. For many years I prayed that I would become more pleasing to God. I feared that I would be ashamed to appear before Christ if I failed to accomplish this vital objective.

But despite my persistent and fervent efforts to become the man I thought God wanted me to be – I always failed. My frustration and discouragement mounted.

Then, finally, I heard a voice within me. The Holy Spirit commanded me to *believe* that God would help me become more pleasing to Him. I realized then that I had been striving to please God on my own, something that I could never accomplish. But I could believe that *He* would make the changes that needed to be made in me.

This revelation inspired the beginning of a new joy within me. By *believing* that God was causing me to grow more pleasing to Him, I was opening my heart ever wider to His joy.

Jesus said, *Apart from me you can do nothing* (Jn. 15:5). He reinforced this even more when He said: *The Son can do nothing by himself; he can do only what he sees his Father doing* (Jn. 5:19).

My prayers to become more pleasing to God had seemed proper at the time, but now I realize that by my own efforts I can do nothing to change my fallen nature. Only God can do that. When I first believed that He would forgive me, and give me His wonderful gift of eternal life, He did. Now He wanted me to believe that He would keep working in me to help me become more like His Son.

When it is difficult for us to believe that God is working in us, we may keep trying harder to make ourselves more pleasing to Him. Then, when we fail, we become frustrated and discouraged. But when we rely on God to make the changes needed in us, our joy and confidence grow. Then we can look forward to standing before Christ's judgment seat, because we know that our faith and confidence is in *Him*, not in ourselves.

God's Perfect Plan

When Jesus was asked what was our most important priority, He said: *First, Love God.* Why would God insist we must love Him before we do anything else? Loving God can be difficult unless we understand *why* we should love Him.

If we try to love God just because He is all-powerful, we may falter. We don't love others because they are much stronger than we are. In fact, we are more likely to be afraid of them.

If we try to love God just because He knows so much more than we do, we are likely to feel intimidated and overwhelmed by His superior intellect.

If we try to love Him because He has always been, and always will be, we end up   confused: How can something have "always been" we ask. "How could that be?"

God knows our inability to love someone we've never seen in person, so He devised His perfect plan: He came to earth as His Son, Jesus.

It's easier for us to love someone if we realize he has suffered for our benefit. And if we know that person loves us exactly as we are, we want to love him in return. Most people who find it difficult to thank God for everything, are caught in a personal struggle: "I love God, but do I love Him enough to trust Him?"

Job, the first book of the Bible to be written, was designed by God to assure us that no matter what happens, He loves us and is always in charge. God permitted trials and tragedies in Job's life. Job suffered the destruction and loss of all he owned, the death of his children, and a painful physical affliction. But in the end he joyfully declared his unwavering faith in God.

Later, Abraham was willing to trudge two thousand

130

miles through the wilderness, not knowing where he was headed, because he trusted God.

Throughout the Bible God admonishes us to trust that He is always working for our good. God offers us His perfect solutions for every problem that you and I will ever have. We can choose to live in fear and unhappiness, or we can trust Him, and enjoy the benefits of knowing that He will always supply exactly what we need.

The Power That Controls

No jury to impress. No judge to persuade. The court trials were over, the juries and judges were gone.

I have sat in many prison cells and listened to inmates as they shared their hearts. Their tragic confessions taught me many things about the intense darkness of the demonic world.

Some prisoners described their inability to understand the horrible things they had done. Some said they couldn't even remember committing their crimes. Other inmates admitted their crimes, but insisted that they had been unable to stop themselves. These tragic accounts convinced me that many of them had been, and still were, under the control of the evil that exists around us.

Many Christians have little perception of that shadowy spiritual world. But it does exist, and we need to know what frightful influence it can have over us.

The common denominator in nearly all these inmates was the activities in which they had been engaged *prior* to committing their crimes. As Peter said in 2 Peter 2:19: *A man is a slave to whatever has mastered him.*

We assume that everyone has the ability to make

their own decisions and control what they do. That may be true in most cases, but to some degree the spiritual realm influences us all. And we choose *which* spiritual power influences us.

If we revel in pornography, the darkness of that evil realm injects itself into our lives. The more we look and enjoy, the stronger the influence it will exert over us. Men in prison for rape and murder have told me that this is so!

If we frequent gambling establishments, the spirit of greed for easy gain can enter our hearts. If we fellowship with the wrong people, the evil spirits that influence them can gradually begin to influence us, too.

Some readers may think the evil spiritual realm is a myth, but the writers of the New Testament knew that it was and is real. Ephesians 6:12 (TLB) says: *We are not fighting against people made of flesh and blood, but against persons without bodies – the evil rulers of the unseen world, those mighty satanic beings and great evil princes of darkness who rule this world; and against huge numbers of wicked spirits in the spirit world.*

The Good News is that the Holy Spirit commands a much more powerful spirit world – the realm of God and righteousness! This world can likewise influence everything we feel, think and do – if we choose to obey our Lord instead of our own sinful nature. Choose to obey God, and He will change your despair into joy!

God's Agenda

The spirit of rebellion has always resided in the human heart. Christians, too, have rebelled against God's way of doing things.

Although we realize that God is perfect, we question His actions when we consider them to be imperfect. How ridiculous! Here we are, absolutely imperfect beings, yet feeling ourselves qualified to determine what a perfect God should do!

For example, we probably don't understand the following: I chose to bless Jacob but not Esau. And God said this before the children were even born, before they had done anything either good or bad. This proves that God was doing what he had decided from the beginning; it was not because of what the children did but because of what God wanted and chose (see Ro. 9:12-13 TLB).

We must also consider verses 14 and 15: *Was God being unfair? Of course not. For God had said to Moses, "If I want to be kind to someone, I will. And I will take pity on anyone I want to".*

Our Creator has His agenda. Rebellion against His Will is not very wise, and is definitely not a way to receive His blessings.

Throughout many of my earlier years I excused my rebellious ways by blaming them on what I considered to be God's unfairness. But eventually I learned that He really does know what is best for each of us.

Jesus said that He could do only what God told Him to do (see Jn. 5:30). As a result, He had power over everything here on earth: people, sickness, weather – even death. To me that says, we should obey God whether or not we understand what He says or does.

Ephesians 5:20 (NKJ) says, *Giving thanks always for all things to God the Father in the name of our Lord Jesus Christ*. Of course, we don't always *feel* like thanking Him for things we don't understand. But when we do, our obedience to His Word opens the way for God to greatly increase our happiness.

The more we walk the path of obedience to God,

the more peace He will give us in everything that happens to us.

God's Intimate Attention

There are people who believe that God created the world, then left it to run its own course. What a bleak and hopeless existence such people must endure.

We know that God has revealed Himself to people throughout history, but we must decide how intimately does He involve Himself in *our* everyday lives. Does He occasionally control what happens to us? Frequently govern the events of our lives? Or is He involved as intimately as the battery that causes a wristwatch to run? Is the slightest most insignificant event, as well as the most important event of each day, under His control?

I believe that the amount and quality of happiness we enjoy is determined by our view of the role God plays in our lives. Jesus said, *He knows the number of hairs on your head!* (Lu. 12:7 TLB).

We can trust in God only to the extent that we believe He is in control of the events that are important to us. If we believe that He is too busy doing other things, then we feel cast off, abandoned. Most of us wouldn't feel very secure in that situation.

First Peter 1:8 gives us the ideal way to view our lives: *Though you have not seen him, you love him; and even though you do not see him now, you believe in him and are filled with an inexpressible and glorious joy.*

Although we don't see God with our eyes, our joy is based on our faith in what He *is now* doing. My conviction is that God is involved in *everything*. Nothing comes our way in life that does not have His intimate attention. Just as a battery-operated watch would stop without a working battery, everything in the universe is dependent upon the power of His Word for its existence. God's involvement in everything that happens to us is at the very heart of our joy. When we doubt His active and intimate participation, our joy plummets.

There are countless times every day when we must decide if God is involved in the events of our life. Is He, or is He not, involved in every detail of our circumstances? If He is involved, then we can fully believe and have confidence in Romans 8:28 (KJV): *We know that all things work together for good to them that love God*.

We should pay special attention to the first two words, "we know." *Knowing* something is true is considerably different than *hoping* something is true. If we *know* that God is involved in every event of our lives and causing them to work for our good, then we have every reason to rejoice in His perfect and loving care for us.

If you have been existing in a bleak world where you think God is only *partially* involved, I urge you to enter into the world that Jesus came to introduce. Jesus believed that *nothing* could happen without God's permission. In fact, He was amazed that people had so little faith in God.

Jesus urges us to live in confidence that His Father is watching over every detail of our lives. Any lack of joy, at any time or in any situation, can be remedied by returning to a faith that God is in control, and that, *In him we live and move and are!* (Ac. 17:28 TLB)

A Cheerful Heart

Rejoice in the Lord always (Ph. 4:4 KJV). Rejoice today! This hour! Right now!

But now may not be our favorite time to rejoice. We may feel more like feeling sorry for ourselves, or feeling angry or tired. Then why would God command us to rejoice always? Does He know things about us that we don't know about ourselves? Of course He does – He's our Creator.

There is a quality in rejoicing that causes it to build a wall around us that protects us from many of Satan's attacks. Satan, the enemy of our happiness, delights in our negative emotions and uses them to infect our spirits.

Rejoicing motivates us to get our minds off our problems and off ourselves. Rejoicing convinces us that, *A cheerful heart is good medicine* (Pr. 17:22).

Rejoicing makes it possible for the Holy Spirit to defeat Satan's attacks and to have greater influence over our spirits! This, in turn, causes our spirits to exercise increased control over our naturally complaining human nature.

When we are upset we can think of an *abundance* of "good" reasons to dwell on unhappy thoughts. This, though, would be a little like someone cutting off his nose to spite his face. He would hurt only himself. In the same way, we hurt only ourselves when we allow Satan to oppress us with unhappiness. Is there a solution? Yes! Rejoice in the Lord – Always! We have nothing to lose but everything to gain.

God knows it is often difficult for us to rejoice in difficult circumstances. He promises, though, to come to our assistance if we will just center our attention on Him and His love for us, rather than on our problems.

Giving Birth to Joy

I will be merciful to their unrighteousness, and their sins and their iniquities will I remember no more (He.

136

8:12 KJV). We humans seem incapable of forgiving and forgetting the transgressions of those who have harmed us. Our fallen nature seems to insist that we carry the memories of their offenses within us. And even if we can *forgive*, we find it almost impossible to forget. Our unhappy thoughts and resentments linger on until they weigh us down like heavy burdens. If only we could rid ourselves of our painful thoughts, and forgive and forget like God does.

If we have spent a lifetime clinging to memories of the ways in which people have wronged us, it can be very difficult for us to turn from those old ways. I know that myself, from painful experience. After clinging to distressing memories for many years, I thought it would be impossible to clear my mind of those unhappy thoughts. But then I learned about God's plan to free us from the pain of other people's actions. And I came to understand that His solution works.

Now whenever I think of someone whom I felt had wronged me, I begin to believe that God used that person to teach me what I needed to learn, and I pray, "God, please bless him." But even that prayer didn't work very well until I began to list some of the good things I wanted God to do for him. Then I thought of even *more* wonderful things that God could do for him. As I did, my painful thoughts began to leave.

I was learning that God would cause other people's actions to increase my happiness, even if that had not been their intention. God was indeed blessing me!

God comforts us by assuring us that He forgives our sins. He also wants to free us from our painful memories. He is not imposing a burden on us when He commands us to forgive others, because He knows that forgiving others will give birth to a new joy in us.

Gradually I came to understand why Jesus said,

Pray for the happiness of those who curse you; implore God's blessing on those who hurt you (Lu. 6:28 TLB).

If *you* have been struggling under the burden of painful memories, now is a wonderful time to believe that God will cause those memories to be turned into new joy.

Joy at the End

I've heard that elderly folks sometimes experience some personality changes as they approach their time of death. They may become irritable, or frightened, and say things that are completely out of character for them. I had often prayed that God would prevent me from being a poor witness for Him as I approach my own departure from this world. I confess, though, that I was still concerned about what the last words to come from my lips might be. That is, until a very meaningful event happened some months ago.

X-rays of my left shoulder revealed that bone spurs were tearing a tendon inside the shoulder. I entered the Surgery Center where the surgeon was to remove the spurs. Mary was with me in the room where I was being prepared for the operation.

The anesthesiologist placed an IV in my arm and told me that I would feel only a slight sting. That was the last thing I heard or remembered until after the surgery.

Even so, I began to speak. Mary told me later that the anesthesiologist looked at me as if surprised that I could still talk. Mary wrote down what I said.

"I know that God is going to use this for my good."

I was quiet for a moment or two, then I said,

"God and I have a covenant – He has promised to make everything work for my good." The doctor gave me another surprised look.

After a few seconds I said:

"My trust is in the Lord." By now the doctor was *quite* surprised that I was still able to talk.

That experience, I believe, was a gift from God. Through it He was revealing the spirit of praise that has been growing in me. Now I'm no longer anxious about what my feelings, attitudes or words may be should my conscious mind no longer control my words.

The spirit of praise is a gift that God wants every Christian to have. No matter how difficult our circumstances may be, a spirit of praise is able to control our natural reactions to them. God permits us to decide the kind of spirit that we want to rule in our hearts. If we allow anxiety or unhappiness to control our thoughts, we will react accordingly during times of crisis.

But through Christ, joy can take root in our hearts and bear wonderful fruit when we need it the most. A fruit tree grows its roots day by day, year by year. Its deep roots tap the water for the nourishment and strength it will need when strong winds blow. Deep-rooted joy causes seeds of praise to grow in our hearts, to enable us to withstand the tempests of life. Begin to plant *your* seeds of joy now, so that in time, you can bask beneath your Tree of Joy!

Expecting Good Things

The bottom could fall out at any time.

The sky could fall.

We could get ill. Our car could quit running. We could lose our job. Our finances could crash. Our children's lives could go badly. Our friends could turn against us.

It's easy for us to live in a state of anxiety, always expecting bad things to happen. In Job, God explained the way things work here on earth. Job said, *What I feared has come upon me; What I dreaded has happened to me* (Job. 3:25).

There are an unlimited number of things that we can worry about. These anxieties can deprive us of the happiness God intends for us to have. That is precisely why Satan is always trying to inject unpleasant thoughts into our minds. But God gives us the authority and ability to reject all such thoughts. We can choose instead to embrace: *Whatever is true, whatever is noble, whatever is right, whatever is pure, whatever is lovely, whatever is admirable- if anything is excellent or praiseworthy-think about such things* (Ph. 4:8).

When our minds are invaded by unpleasant thoughts, God wants us to think about something else. When we obey Him, good things happen.

It's easy for us to adopt the lifelong habit of wasting our time and energy on downcast thoughts. Once in place these negative thoughts can eventually destroy our happiness. The wiles of Satan are so subtle that we may not perceive this process as it occurs. However, there is a solution!

We can make a *deliberate* choice to reject disagreeable thoughts and replace them with those that are *excellent* or *praiseworthy*.

Learning to think pure and noble thoughts does not come easily. It can be so much easier for us to heed Satan rather than God. But when we reject the devil and obey God, the rewards are unlimited. Our minds and spirits radiate a new and ever-abundant joy. If you have not turned your thoughts to the true, the noble, the pure, I urge you to do so now.

Unable to Sleep

We've all endured sleepless nights that seemed to last forever. We've tossed and turned and fretted all night. When morning finally came we've dragged ourselves from bed, convinced that we would have a miserable day. And we did. For many years I permitted myself to spend the following day fretting over my lack of sleep. Those thoughts were not happy, and my body responded by agreeing with my every negative thought. Those days dragged on and on.

Then one day the Holy Spirit interrupted my self-pity and asked me why I had slept so poorly the night before. I listed what I thought were the reasons. Then He asked me if I thought God had had any part in my lack of sleep. My initial response was, *Oh no, He wants us to rest well so we will be healthy*. That seemed reasonable to me. But the Spirit pressed on with Scripture verses about all things working for my good. Why, then, couldn't God use my lack of sleep to do something good for me?

Then the Holy Spirit began to inquire into what I had been doing while I couldn't sleep. Well, I thought, I hadn't prayed for anyone, because all I could think about was going back to sleep. And, no, I hadn't spent that extra time praising the Lord, because I was too tired to think about that. My answers, I know now, were based on a mistaken belief that sleeping well all night is good, and interrupted sleep is bad.

This mistaken belief caused me many years of needless unhappiness, years during which I accepted the spirit of tiredness and felt sorry for myself. But the Holy Spirit changed all that.

Now I greet each day with joy and enthusiasm. Now I know that God wants to use my nights, whether restful or not, for my good and His glory. Now, the day following a restless night takes on a new perspective to me. My thoughts become positive as I rejoice in God's wonderful goodness to me, and my body responds to what I believe.

Sleep is not as critical as we grew up believing it to be. True, we enjoy its healing quality, but there are many things that God wants us to learn, some of which can best be learned while the world around us sleeps. It is during the stillness of the night that God seeks our attention and draws us into prayer and praise.

The night before He was crucified, Jesus knew that His disciples would be faced with a difficult time. He knew that their bodies needed all the strength they could get from a good night's rest. But He also knew they needed *spiritual* strength far more, for soon He would be arrested. They would be tempted to deny that they had ever known Him. For that reason He awakened them twice and urged them to pray:

Couldn't you even stay awake with me one hour? (Mt. 26:49 TLB).

Perhaps Christ is asking us the same question during times of sleeplessness. Let's not miss His call to prayer.

A Smile on the Inside

A smile on our face is valuable. Not only does it help us, it also helps those who encounter us. Jesus affirms this in Luke 6:38: *Give, and it will be given to you.* Giving a smile to others, then, is a good way to increase our own joy!

However, being told to smile when we hurt inside can cause us to be resentful. Most of us, after all, don't like to pretend to be what we are not. What, then, should we do?

The Holy Spirit has the answer: God wants us to *smile on the inside as well as the outside.* Easier said than done? Yes – but the Holy Spirit will help us if we call upon Him.

Once I doubted that the Holy Spirit could change

my sometimes sour disposition. But I kept praying and seeking His guidance. Soon I began to experience small changes in my attitude. I *wanted* to smile, and I felt resentful less often. There was a new spring in my steps, and people started saying, "You seem so much happier than before!" Well, I *was* happier – smiling on the inside. My problems had not changed – I had.

It can be difficult for us to understand what Jesus meant when He said, *only believe*. Those words can be a mystery to us. Our skeptical nature wants to believe in things only *after* we see them. But the Bible says, *Faith is being . . . certain of what we do not see* (He. 11:1).

Children find it easy to believe in what they don't see, but we adults want proof. If we are going to have a smile in our hearts, we want something to smile about. That is why Jesus told us to have a childlike faith, a faith that believes in what is unseen.

Our misunderstanding of what faith is can often cause us to stumble. Imagine a little child learning to walk. Since as yet he has learned only to crawl, learning to walk is a challenge to him. But eventually he *must* learn. Likewise, to become pleasing to God we must *learn* to have faith, even if we have learned only to doubt our entire lives.

Jesus said: *I will ask the Father, and he will give you another Counselor to be with you forever* (Jn. 14:16). The Greek word used for Counselor is "parakletos" also meaning, "helper."

All of us need The Counselor. Life is complicated, with many painful trials to endure. We need help in order to *Rejoice in the Lord always. I will say it again: Rejoice!* (Phil. 4:4). That help is ours for the asking through Christ Jesus.

143

The more I learn to smile on the inside, the more my joy increases. The more I trust the Holy Spirit to help me, the more my faith increases. This is a faith and joy I strongly urge I *you* to seek, a faith and joy based on the promises of Christ Himself.

Helping Others

God created each of us to complete our respective missions. No one else can accomplish our particular assignment.

If we see ourselves as the unique results of God's inspiration, our lives take on new meaning. We are more likely to believe that He involves Himself in every detail of our lives. Even negative people and events can be used by Him to nudge us toward His goals for us.

Some unbelievers insist that we are deceiving ourselves when we believe that God is actively involved in this world. But even if that were so, I've learned that helping others gives us pleasure. Seeing discouraged people receive new hope and joy is among the most satisfying of experiences. God's joy is like a boomerang—it keeps coming back to us when we give it to others.

Jesus said in Luke 6:38: *Give, and it will be given to you.A good measure, pressed down, shaken together and running over, will be poured into your lap.*

When our joy decreases, Proverbs 11:25 gives us a proven remedy: *He who refreshes others will himself be refreshed.*

I once attended a home Bible Study hosted by an 82-year-old man. This elderly gentleman bubbled with such joy and enthusiasm that I gained a new understanding of why God wants us to be joyful. This man made such an impression on me, in fact, that I also attended his Sunday School class, where once again I saw him bring joy to other people. He didn't teach or preach, he just interacted with everyone. His sincere joy and personal warmth were a blessing to others; qualities we should all strive to emulate.

God's joy creates enthusiasm in us, which in turn encourages others to receive His joy. As a result of meeting this man, I'm now more dedicated than ever to proclaiming Christ's joy to all the world.

God's Special Joy

Consider this all-too-familiar scenario:

You are tired, angry, discouraged. Really stressed out. You definitely aren't in the mood for being "super-spiritual". Acting as if you are the picture of joy is not on your agenda. The last thing you want is yet another spiritual exercise.

I understand. I've been there – many times. What to do?

Jesus was a master at devising practical solutions to problems, yet people often brush off His solutions as *not* being practical. When He said that, *Anything is possible if you have faith* (Mk. 9:23 TLB), He meant just that – *anything.*

When we hit a "stone wall" of stress, overwork, anger or dejection, that's the ideal time to practice believing what Jesus taught us. That's the time to believe that God is replacing our unhappiness with His joy. That's when we should believe that with each passing second our inner joy is increasing. In short, we should learn to believe that it is our times of trouble that God uses to create new joy in us.

When we do this, those times become extra special. We experience a joy that doesn't come from completing our work, being entertained, eating an extra special meal, or anything else that normally brings us satisfaction. Those special moments are something like being on an escalator moving upward. We are not moving ourselves. We are being *lifted*.

God has reserved a special joy that comes only as we learn to believe Him. As we believe, we come to understand that our difficulties can be a stairway to His higher calling.

Believe it. God's special inner joy is available to us under *all* circumstances. Each problem we encounter presents yet one more opportunity to learn to believe what He says; each trial we face offers another chance to grow in believing that God is doing whatever He wants done!

The best way I can describe my feelings as I trust in God, is that I have a very intense feeling of thanksgiving to Him, and a keen awareness that He is taking care of all my needs.

Perhaps Psalm 23:4 (KJV) explains it best: *Though I walk through the valley of the shadow of death, I will fear no evil: for thou art with me*.

Fear no evil? Did this writer have any idea of the fears we face as we conduct our daily affairs? Yes, I think he did. I believe he enjoyed a personal knowledge that God was with him and would *always* be with him, even in the face of death. Because of Jesus, we can now enjoy an even happier relationship with God. We will fear no evil for He *is* with us. Such blessed assurance increases our joy when we walk through our own valley of troubles.

The Fires of Joy

There comes a time during our search for the joy of the Lord when we realize that we must suffer. We come to learn, in fact, that there are some facets of joy that come *only* through suffering. Jesus said in John 12:24 (NCV): *A grain of wheat must fall to the ground and die to make many seeds. But if it never dies, it remains only a single seed.* Dying *does* bring a dramatic change to that which once was alive. Dying may not be what we want, of course, but it is what we all need, because that's the way we enter Heaven!

The citizens of Iceland have been described as the happiest people on earth. The winters there are bitterly cold, with darkness reigning for twenty hours each day. To most of us, Iceland does not spell "happiness." A native sociologist there believes that the reason for his people's happiness is not in their comforts, but that their discomforts have convinced them to enjoy what they have!

During my childhood my generation faced many conditions that would likely cause "suffering" to today's young people. When we went anywhere while our dads were working, we traveled by foot or, if we were lucky, by bicycle. We seldom knew the pain of pleading with our parents to take us anywhere. We had plenty of time to fellowship with one another as we walked or ran from place to place. In fact, almost everything we did seemed to produce fun. We seldom got into trouble for being out too late, because home was the only place we could get something to eat! Our parents rarely had difficulty locating us, because they knew the parents of all our friends. And we knew for sure that if we did something wrong, someone in our community would soon tell our parents. Those "sufferings," I know now, helped us to grow up balanced and secure.

Most of us had to work at family chores. Such work was not our preferred activity, but without our knowing it, these chores actually were a blessing to us. We enjoyed simple things, and our nerves were not frayed by the frantic pace of many present day activities.

We can all profit from our difficulties. Countless successful people, in fact, have declared that it was their difficulties that caused them to succeed in life.

How, then, can we cause our difficulties to work for our good? God's Word addresses this question in Romans 5:3 (TLB): *We can rejoice, too, when we run into problems and trials, for we know that they are good for us - they help us learn to be patient.* Understanding that God intends for all things to work for our good will stoke the fires of joy in our hearts.

Spiritual Superiority

When I was young, I did not feel mentally or morally superior to anyone. But that changed when I became a Christian. My zeal to win people to Christ became stronger than that of anyone else I knew. This zeal was a gift from God, but I became prideful and "holier-than-thou". I began to think that other Christians were lax and lazy about spreading the Gospel.

My irrepressible zeal also caused me to look down on those who had been Christians for many years. Even the people who were responsible for helping me to become a Christian seemed to me to be poor examples of what Christians should be.

I thought I was more faithful than most Christians, and I'm sure my inflated opinion of myself was obvious to others! When I had the opportunity to preach at my home church, I found ways to point out the sins I saw in some of the members. It never occurred to me to thank those dear people for what they had done to help me become a Christian. A feeling of superiority nearly always makes us think more highly of ourselves than we ought to think.

Later my high opinion of myself turned to sorrow as I learned painful lessons about my own feet of clay.

Now I look forward to the time when I will see those dear saints in Heaven, and can thank them for all their prayers and efforts on my behalf.

The following verses have become increasingly important to me: *All of you, clothe yourselves with humility toward one another, because God opposes the proud but gives grace to the humble. Humble yourselves, therefore, under God's mighty hand, that he may lift you up in due time* (1 Pe. 5:5-7).

I have learned that God withholds many good things from us if we entertain pride. Once we feel superior to other people we remove ourselves from the protection of "God's mighty hand." We then become prime targets for Satan's temptations.

The more I learn about humility, the more clearly I see how far I have often strayed from God's Will. I realize His amazing grace in all He has done for me. As I meditate on His patient love for each of us, my joy in Him continues to increase.

Ugly Bugs

When we hurt we are very likely to wonder why God doesn't help us. At those times we may be the closest we have ever been to doubting that the God of the Bible exists. During long, sleepless nights we may suffer more than we thought we could endure. We may think, *If were God, I would help anyone who hurts this badly.*

There is a scripture that I cling to when I am severely tested. First Corinthians 10:13 says, *No temptation has seized you except what is common to man. And God is faithful; he will not let you be tempted beyond what you can bear. But when you are tempted, he will also provide a way out so that you can stand up under it.*

When we suffer we are being tempted, tested and tried. We are tested in ways that are similar to what Job, Paul and Peter experienced. If we learn to be victorious in these tests, in Heaven we will be able to fellowship with those who also wrestled with and were victorious over these same problems.

We may be tempted to think, *I don't care about being victorious. What I want is to be delivered from this problem*. This is the moment when we have the opportunity and greatest need to enter into new joy through our faith in Christ.

In the college I attended, a Biology student was assigned the project of catching a bug and writing a research report on it. She searched diligently for an *attractive* bug to study, but the only bug to be found was small, black and definitely ugly. *What an ugly bug!* she thought. But when viewed under the lab microscope, the bug showed its true colors. What had appeared to be ugly was actually beautifully iridescent. What a difference one's perspective can make!

The small or huge "ugly bugs" that inhabit our lives may seem to have no earthly value. We may wish we could get rid of them since we don't understand or appreciate them. But God does, and He is able to turn them into instruments of joy as we trust Him to do so.

Powerful Thoughts

Isaiah 55:8 (NAS) tells us, *My thoughts are not your thoughts, neither are your ways my ways, declares the LORD*. How much influence do our thoughts have over our "ways"?

Consider this illustration: If we think about chocolate cake, the thought was probably caused by our previous relationships with chocolate cake. If those were happy experiences, our next thought may be, *I think I'll get some chocolate cake.* Thoughts often lead to actions.

An artist would tell you that his frame of mind determines how he will paint. If he is sad, his thoughts and feelings will reveal themselves in his paintings. If he is happy, there will be a quality of happiness in his choice of colors and brush strokes. This is why artists urge their students to prepare their minds before they even pick up a brush.

The Bible gives us valuable insights into the kinds of thoughts we should think if we want joy to be a major part of our lives. If we think positive, happy thoughts, subsequent circumstances will reflect those thoughts. Conversely, negative thoughts will almost invariably lead to negative consequences.

You may have heard the expression, "If we keep doing what we did, we'll keep getting what we got!" This maxim speaks to the way of life that I recommend to you. If you believe your life is not following a pattern of ever-increasing joy, try changing your thoughts. Otherwise your life will continue the way it has been going. Psalms 47:1 (NAS) offers this good suggestion: *Clap your hands, all peoples; shout to God with the voice of joy.*

Place this verse in a convenient place where you will see it often. Meditate on its message. A "voice of joy" reflects our faith in God. It is a declaration that we believe we are victorious in Christ. This victorious spirit then turns our apparent defeats into triumphs. I have seen this happen myself, many times. I enthusiastically recommend that *you* embrace a joy-ous spirit.

Make everyone rejoice who puts his trust in you. Keep them shouting for joy . . . Fill all who love you with your happiness (Ps. 5:11 TLB).

Of course, no one feels like "shouting for joy" all

the time. Why, then, would God ask us to do so? Because it is our trust in Him, (as demonstrated by our joyful shouts), that *causes* happiness!

A soldier seldom feels like shouting when he is charging an enemy – he might get killed! But commanders know that when charging soldiers shout, they can often cause the enemy to flee – and that may save the soldiers life!

If we follow God's admonitions, what happens? We open the way for Him to work a transformation in us. We are, by our actions, inviting Him to change us. When people abandon their unhappy thoughts, those who know them often say things such as, "What has happened to you? You used to act so unhappy. Now you look so cheerful." And they are right! God *does* change us when we trust Him instead of worrying about our problems! Trust Him and His happiness will replace your unhappiness.

Incredible Thoughts

If we are in Texas and want to go to New York, but travel in the direction of Los Angeles, we will not reach New York. Likewise, if we want to be joyful, we will not reach that objective if we move in the wrong direction.

If we think our unhappy thoughts are the *result* of our unpleasant circumstances, we may be wrong. Our unhappy thoughts often *cause* our problems. Our thoughts are very powerful, and can change our appearance – even our physical strength.

You may have heard the story about the man who was repairing a flat tire when the jack slipped and the car fell on his child. The desperate father had only one thought: I must save my child! The man then lifted the corner of the car and saved his child. Later, four strong men struggled to pick up the same weight!

Having a close and loving relationship with God will be difficult until we understand how important our thoughts are to Him. Others may see us as someone with certain physical characteristics, but God sees our *thoughts.* To Him, our thoughts are who we are.

The thoughts we think give birth to the person we are! For example, if we think about how angry we are at someone, we can become consumed with that anger. Our facial expressions will then reflect those thoughts.

God has given us the unique ability to control what we think. But if we allow people or situations to control our reactions and emotions, we become slaves to the actions of others.

But now we can break out of that bondage, and declare: *Thanks be to God! He gives us the victory through our Lord Jesus Christ* (1 Co. 15:57).

If people or problems have battered us into being unhappy, discouraged and angry victims of circumstances, we can change! It might be a difficult process, but it *can* be done. Bible verses are a powerful aid.

Think of yourself as mounting up, *on wings like an eagle* (Is. 40:31).

Think of yourself as being made a new person: *When someone becomes a Christian, he becomes a brand new person inside. He is not the same anymore. A new life has begun!* (2 Co. 5:17 TLB).

Sound impossible? God has challenged us to become happy people, overcomers who are not chained to what we have been in the past. We don't *have* to be unhappy just because we always have been. God's Good News shows us a different way. In 2 Corinthians 8:2, Paul writes about New Testament Christians who were having severe trials yet their hearts overflowed with joy.

New Testament Christians certainly knew what problems were! But they learned how to be joyful despite their circumstances. Their happiness then caused them to convince unbelievers that something wonderful had happened within them.

We can be living testaments to what Christ came to do in us. But for that to happen, we must think new thoughts: *Fix your thoughts on what is true and good and right. Think about things that are pure and lovely, and dwell on the fine, good things in others. Think about all you can praise God for and be glad about* (Ph. 4:8 TLB).

Think good and true thoughts, and God will use them to destroy any unhappiness that has attached itself to you. You may think this a formidable task, but persevere, and your rewards will be unlimited!

Good Luck?

Consider the idea of "luck." Many people seek after good luck. Once that thought pattern is established, they may repeatedly look for evidence that good luck is following them.

But once we accept the idea that good luck is possible, we automatically accept the opposite: bad luck. And once we accept the idea of bad luck, we embrace it as *a reality.*

Every year, people in our country spend billions of dollars on gambling. They foolishly seek the elusive favors of "Lady Luck". But she is no lady. She brings with her the fear of *bad* luck. If we believe in luck, we dread the unexpected. We believe that events are out of God's control. Circumstances that seem to be bad luck can drain away our joy.

The measure of joy in our lives will often be determined by our understanding of how actively God involves Himself in everything that happens on this earth. Is He *never* involved, s*ometimes* involved or *always* involved in what happens? Ultimately, what we *believe* determines how we will react to each thing that happens to us.

If you are uncertain of what you believe, I suggest that you study the book of Job. Satan hated Job, and wanted to make him suffer. But before he could afflict Job, he had to obtain God's permission.

Was Job a victim of bad luck? Or was God in control of his circumstances? Were Job's afflictions an exception to God's normal ways of working in our lives? No, they weren't, for in many ways the Bible indicates that God is *always* a part of everything that happens to us. He stops what He wants to stop and He permits what He wants to permit. He allows some things to happen that we feel *we* would *never* allow. And He stops other things from happening that we think *should* occur.

God gives us the opportunity to trust in *Him,* rather than in our own judgment. No matter how much we may disagree with Him, we must decide if we believe that He is all wise and altogether loving toward mankind.

There is no such thing as good luck or bad luck. We would be foolish to look to or depend on them. Luck is not a part of our Christian heritage. Christ has promised to provide *all that we need* (see Ph. 4:19).

Joy stays with us when we believe that God is totally involved in our lives (see Je. 29:11, Ps. 40:5). We rejoice as we sing, "God is working for my good." And we see ever increasing evidence of His presence. God honors the faith of those who believe He is always working for their good, and increases their joy!

For Such a Time as This

The vast kingdom of Persia stretched from India to Ethiopia. Every Jew in that immense empire was scheduled to be executed. One woman, Esther, had the potential to save them. But to do so she would have to risk own her life. Mordecai challenged her: *Who knows, you may have been chosen queen for just such a time as this!* (Es. 4:14 NCV).

Each of us has come to where we are "for such a time as this."

Esther took the necessary risk and saved her people. You and I may face a different challenge, but a challenge it is. *Our struggle is not against flesh and blood, but against the rulers, against the authorities, against the powers of this dark world and against the spiritual forces of evil in the heavenly realms* (Ep. 6:12).

These unseen forces are always seeking ways to defeat God's people. They use both our circumstances and other people in their efforts to influence us (see Mt. 16:23). It is essential, then, that we be aware that we are in our position as God's children for such a time as this. We may be able to help just one person, or we may be able to help many people. The important thing is that we be faithful wherever God has placed us.

I've been asked many times, "How can I know what God wants me to do?" One answer is in Judges 9:33: *Do whatever your hand finds to do.*

We often dislike the opportunities we have. We often feel that our lives would be easier and happier if our circumstances were different. But if we continue to think this way, we will miss the opportunities as well as the rewards that God wants to give us.

We can find great joy when we realize that God has placed us here, at this time and place, to accomplish our assigned mission. As I look back on my many years here on earth, I realize that my most difficult experiences have been used by God to mold my life. Even though I often complained at the time, God knew that there were things I needed to learn!

You have the opportunity to learn things that can be only learned in your particular situation. If God has not provided a way for you to improve your circumstances, believe that He calls you to serve Him where you are. You can *Serve the Lord with gladness* (Ps. 100:2 KJV).

When you do, your rewards and your joy will be great.

Do People Dislike You?

Do you ever wonder what it would be like if everyone gave you the recognition and respect that you would like?

Would you feel better about yourself, and be happier, if you knew that everyone had only good thoughts about you?

As it is now, you may feel that people in authority probably would not even accept a telephone call from you. They don't know who you are, and maybe couldn't care less. Would all of that change if suddenly everyone understood your abilities and your desire to be helpful?

Perhaps it would help you if you realized that many people feel they aren't accepted and given the respect they believe they deserve. As a result, they sometimes try to impress others by their appearance or material possessions so people will admire them more.

We may never understand why people evaluate us

as they do, but that should not be our primary concern. Whether they rank us above or below what we deserve isn't the point. What we *should* believe is that regardless of what people think about us, God will cause their thoughts to work for our good. Shouldn't that confidence give us joy?

We have been trained throughout our lives to do whatever we can do to impress people. At home, school and work we are always being evaluated. Getting along well with others is a good characteristic, but being burdened by what they think of us is *not* good.

We can know that God brings different people into our lives in order to accomplish His purposes. Some people will love us, but others will . . . well, you name it. We can believe that those people who despise us were selected by God to test and try us.

Sometimes it helps to consider the way people responded to Jesus. Here was God Himself in their midst – the Perfect, Pure, Holy One. But He was hated, rejected, and ultimately, put to death. You and I certainly aren't up to *His* level of perfection! If anything, then, we should expect *worse* treatment than that suffered by Him.

Matthew 10:25 says: *It is enough for the student to be like his teacher, and the servant like his master.*

Most Christians want to become more like Jesus. Jesus never tried to gain people's approval, and often said and did things that made people dislike, even despise Him. He was so consumed with being what *God* wanted Him to be that people's opinions did not move Him. So there we have it – if we become more like Jesus, we will be less influenced by people's thoughts toward us. The more we take on His nature, the greater our joy becomes.

The more we strive to be like Jesus, the more we

can find joy in whatever others think about us, whether good or bad. You may think that such a high goal is too difficult to reach, but try it, and the Holy Spirit will help you. Be assured, too, that God will provide you with the fullness of His joy in the midst of anything that is going on in your life.

Prepared as God's Witnesses

In Acts 5:32 (NKJ) Peter said: *We are witnesses of these things.* Those with serious problems don't want to hear someone with small problems tell them how to become a Christian.

Such people are usually more influenced by Christians who have big problems, yet still cling to a strong faith in God. Sometimes the more severe the believer's problem is, the more likely it is that the unbeliever will listen to him. For example, a son who has ignored his mother's faith for many years may kneel by her side and ask for her prayers when he knows she is dying. Men in prison will listen more attentively to someone who has suffered the same punishment.

Preparing ourselves to be God's witnesses can sometimes be painful, but He wants believers to demonstrate an unwavering faith that will move the heart of an unbeliever.

Job endured much suffering, but he persevered and received high praise from God. Multitudes have considered Job's experiences and have been inspired to believe in and put their trust in God.

Paul suffered in prison. Many thousands of prisoners have since studied his writings and decided they too should follow God.

You and I are God's special messengers to the unbeliever. We can show them that no matter what He permits in our lives, we are positive God loves us and is supplying what we need.

We may be in a place where we think no one will ever see our faithfulness to God, but our witness is *never* in vain. At the right time He will cause our light to shine for some lost person who can see Christ only in the person that we are. He or she will see and hear the witness that we are through our faith in Him. God can use our testimony just as effectively as He has that of Job, Paul, and so many others.

Our journey here on earth is our big moment on God's stage. The parts we play will culminate at the conclusion of our lives on Planet Earth. Some of us may be stagehands, while others are leading actors. Ultimately, however, we each play the role God has chosen for us, to complete His perfect plan. Believing this gives us confidence that He is using our lives to help those for whom Jesus died. What could give us greater joy?

Secret Joy

I understood it – quite by accident. Or maybe it was by design.

I did something to help a person I didn't know, who didn't know me, and whom I didn't expect to see again. Suddenly I felt something new. Maybe this is what Jesus meant when He said, *If you do good to those who are good to you, what credit is that to you? Even 'sinners' do that* (Lu. 6:33).

When I looked back over my life, I realized how often I had expected something in return for what I did for people. We *expect* someone to respond favorably to our acts of kindness. We believe people should at least thank us if we treat them well.

If we give money to a worthy cause, we expect a "thank you." If we pleasantly hold the door open for someone, we expect them to smile, nod their heads, or say something. If they don't, we can feel resentful and even wish that we hadn't helped the ungrateful soul.

If we have been fair with people, we expect them to be fair with us. We are happy if others practice "turn about is fair play." But Jesus gave us a new principle, and a new way to feel His joy. *Your reward will be great, and you will be sons of the Most High, because he is kind to the ungrateful and wicked* (Lu. 6:35).

I was feeling that "reward"! Jesus showed us the way, but it seems to take some of us a lifetime to understand. When that little light turned on in me, I began to seek opportunities to do things for people when I expected to receive nothing in return. Each time that light in me became brighter. No one else knew what a person named Merlin had done, but *I* knew. That secret knowledge caused joy to keep increasing within me.

Maybe it's difficult to find ways to do things secretly for others, but it's often easy to do things for people when they don't expect us to do so. We can do more than our share. More than we have done in the past. The important point here is that we should *expect nothing in return*. Our previous expectations must be denied if we want to experience the secret joy that Jesus offers us. And this is a joy that no one can take from us.

The Law of Believing

Unhappiness is the Devil's tool. It sometimes causes people to become alcoholics or drug addicts. It can destroy families and cause countless other miseries. Sometimes when people do wrong things they excuse themselves by claiming "unhappiness."

We all feel its powerful influence. It can pull every human toward its bottomless pit.

There is no end to unhappiness. The more of it we suffer, the stronger its destructive power. The more we indulge its insatiable appetite to control us, the more ravenous it becomes.

God saw the misery that unhappiness had unleashed on His creation, so He provided a new power on earth to rescue men from sadness. Jesus came to show us the way to eternal life and everlasting joy (see Is. 35:10).

Jesus offered the gift of peace to those who believe, but His peace requires strict adherence to the law of believing. When we believe, we have it. But if we concentrate on our circumstances, we will continue to wrestle with our doubts and unhappiness.

Satan, the evil creator of unhappiness, never gives up. He offers – no, he pushes – his unhappiness on anyone who will accept it.

Happiness is a *choice* that is open to anyone. But *we* must make that choice. Unhappiness is something like the heavy smoke in a burning building. If we breathe the smoke into our lungs, we suffer. In the same way, if we surrender to unhappiness we suffer.

I wasted a big portion of my life wallowing in the pit of unhappiness. I always thought I was unhappy because of my *circumstances*. Now I realize how foolish I was. There I was, with good eyesight, excellent hearing, a strong body, freedom, good health – and still unhappy! God's goodness was indeed wasted on me.

Now I understand that the blessings we have are not enough to create lasting happiness. We must believe that God *wants* to work for our good in every situation. Then we can receive His joy *regardless* of what is going on in our lives. God answered the problem of unhappiness through His Son, Jesus. If we trust Him, our circumstances will no longer have the power to control us. Jesus does not impose His joy on us, He simply secured the supply, and said, *Now ask and keep on asking and you will receive, so that your joy* (gladness, delight) *may be full and complete* (Jn. 16:24 AMP).

Jesus told blind men to *believe* if they wanted to see. How could anyone believe they could see if they were blind? But they did believe. And *then* they saw!

You and I may find ourselves in similarly impossible situations, but Jesus would still say to us: *Ask and you will receive.*

The Unhappy Ones

I'm unhappy.

Now, what put that idea into my mind?

Was it the weather? But my neighbor may be delighted with the weather. He may even have prayed for it.

Is it the fact that I just lost my job? But maybe the man who wasn't fired is delighted that I lost my job, instead of him.

One person happy, the other unhappy. What causes us to make the choice to be the unhappy one?

Is it because we don't get what we want? If so, we probably have made that same choice many times. Can we choose to be *happy* even when we *don't* get what we want?

Yes, it's a little like throwing a switch on or off. We can decide to be happy about one thing, but unhappy about another. But we also have the potential to believe that *everything* that happens to us can be a source of joy. We can choose to believe that, *All things work together for good to them that love God* (Ro. 8:28 KJV).

Of course, such a choice isn't easy to make. Such a choice seems contrary to our human nature. But Jesus commands us to do other difficult things, too. He said: *Love your enemies! Pray for those who persecute you!* (Mt.5:44 TLB).

These are not "normal" behaviors! They can be extremely difficult to obey. But if we choose to follow Christ's commands, we are promised: *The peace of God, which surpasses all understanding* (Ph. 4:7 NKJ).

If we do not have that kind of peace, we can make the bold decision to believe that God is *always* working for our good.

Sometimes God responds quickly to our decision, and rewards our hearts with His joy. At other times He tests our sincerity and determination. Sometimes we may think that we are getting no results, and then suddenly realize, "Hey, something good *has* been happening to me, and I didn't even notice it!"

Make the choice to believe that God will *make* your problems work for your benefit. Trusting God's promises gives us rest from the stresses of life.

He Knew What He was Doing

Babies are so adorable that nearly everyone treasures them. We love to see their smiles, and to hear their innocent gurgling sounds. We forgive their faults, and we love to tell them how precious they are. They seem to *know* when we are pleased by their presence.

But what about adults? Do *they* feel loved and likeable? Unfortunately, no. We do not all feel as if we are likeable. In fact, my experience in counseling people, reading their letters and talking with them, is that nearly all of us feel that we are not likeable.

Maybe this feeling begins during the teenager years. Many teens will do almost anything to secure their place as popular members of the "in" crowd. Some will go to great pains to ensure that their peers approve of their clothing. Some will consume alcohol and take drugs, even when that is not what they really want to do, just so other young people will accept them. They may even join a gang, and commit crimes, just so their associates will not reject them as sissies.

College students are a bit more subtle with their yearning to be liked, but they, too, can fall prey to this same passion. When they feel unloved or unliked, they may abandon their moral values.

Even most adults struggle with the same feeling of never being quite likeable enough. There is much reason for us to cheer up, however, for we are not alone! Even though people seldom admit that they don't feel very likeable, they carry this painful thought in their hearts.

But ultimately this human characteristic is of great benefit to us. It causes us to conduct ourselves more appropriately than we otherwise would. Even if we feel irritable, we will restrain our inner passions, and treat others as they should be treated. At the same time, however, we may feel burdened with our thoughts of unhappiness.

If we want others to like us, the chances are good that many will. Our desire to be appreciated may draw some people to us. That doesn't mean that *everyone* will be drawn to us, of course. What we all must learn is that the very nature of our personalities will attract some people but repel others. That doesn't mean that there is something wrong with us. Rather, the problem may lie within them.

God created each of us with a unique personality.

He knew what He was doing when He painstakingly designed us.

We may believe that God created us as we should be, but that we have so bungled our life that it is our fault if everyone seems to dislike us. Yes, sometimes it *is* our own fault, but the truth is that most people are so involved in their own feelings that they aren't sure *how* they feel about other people. They may have strong negative feelings about a few people, but strong positive feelings about an equal number of others. Most of us encounter a vast number of people who don't affect us in *any* way. We think of them as "peripheral people," and they probably think the same about us.

Why, then, should we trouble ourselves with feelings of being unlikable? We should not. We should rejoice that God loves us, and we should be glad that He has given us the desire to be a likeable person. We can then go on to do our best, and let Him take care of all the rest. He will. And He will bless us abundantly because we have decided to trust Him to mold our lives as He sees fit.

There are billions of people on earth from whom God could choose to bring into our lives. We can be sure that some of them will not like us. Some of them will tempt us to doubt God's careful plan for our experiences. We will love some and dislike others. But each person God brings into our lives helps to mold us into the person *He wants to be with* for eternity. Our increased confidence in the perfect ways of God will cause joy to rise up within us.

We are able to hold our heads high no matter what happens and know that all is well, for we know how dearly God loves us, and we feel this warm love everywhere within us because God has given us the Holy Spirit to fill our hearts with his love (Ro.5:5).

Whenever We Hurt

We walk by faith, not by sight (2 Co. 5:7 KJV). Or as "The Living Bible" translates it, *We know these things are true by believing, not by seeing.*

When we face being thrown to the lions because of our Christian faith, that would *not* be a good time for us to begin learning how to walk by faith, rather than by sight! Paul learned to "find joy in" being beaten, whipped and stoned. His was a *real* walk by faith, but how do *we* learn to do it?

Our physical bodies would not find much comfort in our declarations of faith if they were being stoned or burned in a fiery furnace. They would demand that Airborne Division develop gangrene in their feet. This grave affliction was caused by wet, cold feet, and sometimes resulted in their losing toes, even a foot. Men knew they were responsible for the care of their feet, but they sometimes were "too tired, too cold" or didn't think gangrene would happen to them.

It's easy to neglect the proper care of our bodies and then be forced to suffer the consequences. But there is another part of our bodies that we often neglect – our brains. When mistreated, a "gangrene of the brain" can set in. One way to damage the brain is to ignore Philippians 4:8: *Whatever is true, whatever is noble, whatever is right, whatever is pure, whatever is lovely, whatever is admirable–if anything is excellent or praiseworthy–think about such things.*

If uncared for, the brain can spend most of its life dwelling on unpleasant things. This can cause us to lose our health, as well as our happiness. Monitor your thoughts many times a day and you may be surprised to discover how much of your time is spent nursing unhappy thoughts. Paul must have experienced this problem, but then God got his attention and inspired him to give us the solution. We are to think about things that are *true, noble, right, pure, lovely, admirable, excellent* and *praiseworthy.* Such thoughts are designed by God to give us joy. They are God's remedy for health in body, soul and spirit.

Put Philippians 4:8 on a card and carry it with you. Refer to it often as you monitor your thoughts. It can help insure that you don't succumb to "gangrene of the brain!"

Receiving From God

Let us not become weary in doing good, for at the proper time we will reap a harvest if we do not give up (Ga. 6:9). Helping others has the potential to leave us exhausted. We *want* to help people, but we may also become burdened with the weight of all the good things we are trying to do. We call this "burn-out."

Perhaps we wish people would appreciate the things we do for them. Maybe we wish we could have more free time to ourselves. For whatever reason, doing worthy tasks can weigh us down – until we learn to turn the temptation to be weary into *joy.*

It can be done. In fact, we can never do our best at "doing good" until we know for *whom* we are working.

Working for people? Now *that* will often cause us problems. People – all people – will eventually disappoint us. Even people we try to help will sometimes say or express in some way, "Why don't you do more for me?" Or, "You are just doing this to make yourself feel good." Such statements as these can ruin a perfectly good day!

When we hear such ungracious responses to our efforts, it needs to be very clear in our minds that, *Whatever good thing each one does, this he will receive back from the Lord* (Ep. 6:8 NASB).

It is imperative, too, that we know the source of our joy. If we understand that our primary objective is to serve God, then we should get upset only if *He* does not appreciate our efforts.

God promises us abundant rewards for our service to Him. If we seek our rewards from people instead, we will nearly always feel used or overwhelmed.

Using our time, energy and resources to serve people instead of God is often a carefully laid trap devised by our enemy. But the Bible teaches us to minister to others as our service to God.

Jesus explains in Matthew 25:40: *Whatever you did for one of the least of these brothers of mine, you did for me.* Service that is performed as unto the Lord does not produce frustration. Tiredness, perhaps, but not that unpleasant feeling of annoyance.

Remember! *Serve the Lord with gladness*. In this way our service may produce more joy in *us* than it does those persons we serve!

Bad Weather

For most of our lives we have been "trained" to complain whenever the weather is not what we want it to be. Unsatisfactory weather can be the main subject of discussion if enough people are unhappy about it.

Our training in complaining can cause us to begin our days grumbling, "Oh no, not another day of this!" In time we can reinforce this attitude by complaining more and more, then pass along our habit to those who haven't yet become as proficient as we are.

We may not think that this type of grumbling has any spiritual connection. After all, what harm could it possibly do? Lots!

One complaint leads to another, and yet another,

and fretting soon becomes a way of life. But even one complaint, about anything, is sure to have ramifications.

God has called us to be uncomplaining people. He doesn't descend on us with wrath if we complain, but He does reserve special blessings for those who learn to "rejoice always."

Many years ago God began to teach His people what He wanted of them, and it is our responsibility to ponder and learn from those lessons. When the Israelites were thirsty and wailed about their lack of water, God, of course, took note of their sobbing. Then they complained that the food He provided wasn't tasty enough.

Finally, this was the result: *The Lord heard their complaining and was very angry. He vowed that not one person in that entire generation would live to see the good land he had promised their fathers* (De. 1:34-35 TLB).

We may be so used to hearing people complain that we just don't understand why God would consider it such a severe sin. But we need to pay close attention to the above verse, and strive to reduce our complaining to an absolute minimum. In time, perhaps we can cease our complaining altogether.

We can learn to *rejoice* about the weather. How can we do that if we don't like the weather? We can consider the source of the weather. It was God who designed our world, and He knew exactly what the weather would be from the day we were born until the day we die. If we think of Him as the source, we can then rejoice in His wisdom. We can make all weather conditions a matter of praise to God. If we are going to praise Him for environmental factors that we like, we can *learn to like* whatever He decides is best for us.

For example, inclement weather may keep some

folks off the highway, where they might injure themselves or others. If we are trusting God to provide exactly what is needed, we will be delivered from complaining. This will result in new blessings for us from God!

Learning to trust God to do whatever is best for us opens the door for the Holy Spirit to lead us into increased faith. And increased faith will *always* increase our joy. I'm in favor of that. I hope you are too.

In everything you do, stay away from complaining (Ph. 2:14 TLB).

Whatever Works

Although it sometimes takes parents a while to figure it out, most parents know that when children want their way they will do "whatever works." These precious but conniving children inherited this nature from our distant grandparents, Adam and Eve.

Satan works the same devious "whatever works" system against all of us. That is why he attacks us in such specific ways. Satan knows what upsets us, makes us feel alone, wounded or unloved, and what diminishes our joy. Since his scheme works so well, why should he change it?

But we can *learn* to defeat Satan's tactics. It's not always easy to learn how, but once we do, we are on the threshold of new happiness.

Many people follow a never-ending cycle of distress upon distress. They think, *Why do I have such rotten luck?* Or, *Why doesn't God help me?* We need to know how to deal with Satan's very cunning blueprint for making us miserable. He wants to train us to react to *him*, rather than to *God.*

It's helpful to understand what Satan thinks about humans. He is far more clever and cunning than any of us. He considers us so far beneath him that he does not hesitate to use us in whatever way *he* sees fit. He wants to manipulate us in order to disrupt God's plan for us – just as he unsuccessfully tried to manipulate Jesus.

Satan wants to do whatever he knows will make us unhappy. To him it's as simple as dangling a carrot in front of a donkey. *He* manipulates and *we* react.

That is, until that glorious day when we realize who we are – the sons and daughters of God! Then we can stand up on the inside and declare our victory in Christ. Then we will no longer let anger or self-pity control us. We will proclaim to ourselves, to others and to God, that He *is* continually working for our good. We will know that whatever happens to us is exactly what God will use to bring about something valuable for us. When we do this, we will understand the promise of Christ when He said, *It will be done just as you believed it would* (Mt. 8:13).

When we believed that Satan's schemes were ruining our lives, they did. Now, as we believe Christ's promises, *they* operate for us!

People who were once controlled by what other people said or thought about them, the actions of their spouses or employers, how unfairly the government operated, their health, etc., begin to experience a new joy. They no longer see themselves as victims, but as heirs of the promises of God. God's plan for each of us is a life of *victory* rather than defeat.

Remember what Job said? *What I feared has come upon me; what I dreaded has happened to me* (Jb. 3:25). When Job was afraid, he was a victim. When he learned to say, *Though he slay me, yet will I hope in him* (Jb. 13:15), he became a man who could not be defeated by his circumstances.

Peter told us what to do: *Be careful – watch out*

for attacks from Satan, your great enemy. He prowls around like a hungry, roaring lion, looking for some victim to tear apart (1 Pe. 5:8 TLB). Satan takes great delight in convincing people that he doesn't even exist. If we do acknowledge his existence, he then tries to make us believe that we are unable to resist his suggestions. When a lion roars it often paralyzes its intended victim, and that is why Satan strives to make us feel helpless against his temptations! Life is an ongoing opportunity to prove that Jesus came to set the captives free. We were once easily manipulated by temptations and problems, but now we can be free in Christ!

Just as Satan does whatever it takes to discourage us, *we* must do whatever it takes to live the lives of victory that Jesus has provided us. And we have the mighty Holy Spirit of God to help us! The more you *believe* His promises, the greater the joy you will *feel* working in you.

Tired of Struggling

If we are drowning in problems and "going down for the last time," how can we be happy if we feel God *isn't* helping us?

That's easy. We haven't sunk yet!

The disciples had many reasons to trust Jesus, but on one occasion He left them to struggle alone, and for so long, they were convinced that He wasn't going to help them.

At about 6 p.m. the previous day, Jesus had sent them off in a boat before He went up into the mountains to pray. They were experienced fishermen and sailors, but on this night they were struggling with strong and contrary winds.

Jesus had told them where to go (see Mt. 14:22).

He knew that they were struggling and afraid, yet He calmly left them to their plight.

Have you ever felt like God was failing to help you? Have you ever let yourself doubt His faithfulness toward you? Have you ever wondered if it was *His* fault that you were worn down by your problems?

The terrified disciples were nearing exhaustion. For hours they had struggled against relentless winds. They felt helpless and feared their strength would soon give out. They were afraid their boat and their lives would soon be claimed by the angry sea. They most assuredly weren't rejoicing, and they certainly didn't believe that God was working for their *good*!

Finally Jesus appeared, *walking on the water* (see Mt. 14:25). But even this didn't reassure them. They were terrified by what they thought was a ghost. When we are afraid, we don't want a ghost or spirit. We want a strong right arm to reach out and rescue us.

When you and I are in trouble, we want God to *do something*. We may not be in the mood to trust Him, to sing or rejoice. Why should we pretend to be super spiritual when we are just plain scared?

Why? Because Jesus assures us, *Surely I am with you always* (Mt. 28:20).

True or not true? Is it worth trusting Him when we are sinking – when our family or friends are sinking? Just how far *do* we go in believing that He is with us?

To the end! To the very end – and beyond. If we die, we can then challenge Him with, "Where were You?"

No, I don't think we will. As the old song goes, "We will understand it better by and by." One thing is sure: if we die trusting Him, He will not say, *You of little faith . . . why did you doubt?* (Mt. 14:31).

Rather, He will say, *Well done, good and faithful*

servant . . . come and share your master's happiness (Mt. 25:21).

People beset by many problems may become angry when we talk about joy. But the Bible contains 238 verses that speak of joy, and hundreds of others that relate to it. This should leave us no doubt that God really does want us to be happy.

On the Brink of Victory

Let me bring you this complaint: Why are the wicked so prosperous? Why are evil men so happy? (Je. 12:1 TLB).

Ungodly people often *are* happy – sometimes even more so than Christians. How can this be? We may often ask God such questions as this.

I've seen the wicked prosper, but I've also seen them ruin their lives. They do wonderfully well as long as things go their way. But when they lose money, family or health, they often become bitterly unhappy. They blame God, family, friends or life in general. They then create even more problems for themselves, and an infinite number of difficulties for other people.

Regardless of how happy unbelievers may seem to be at the moment, they live on the brink of disaster. Satan may shove them over the edge at any moment. No matter how carefree they may seem, I would never want to be in their shoes.

Yes, Christians do have problems, but we live on the "brink" of new victories. God permits us to be maneuvered into corners where we will learn to trust Him. He says, *I know the plans I have for you. They are plans for good and not for evil, to give you a future and a hope* (Je. 29:11 TLB).

As unbelievers, we often expected bad things to come our way. But now we must stop that old and improper way of thinking. As Christians, we should always anticipate the good that God is preparing for us. Expecting God's goodness is growing in faith.

But what if our lives seem always to be going from bad to worse? If we believe that, we may be under the delusion that God isn't keeping His promises. There is, however, a different way for us to believe!

God wants us to believe that every plan He has for us is good, and that whatever He permits today is in preparation for the good that is to come.

Needless Unhappiness

No one likes to make mistakes. They embarrass us. We may laugh when others make mistakes, but our own are . . . well, different.

We would like to be physically and spiritually perfect. We want to be better than we are, or can be. When we aren't, we may sink into all kinds of depression.

God built within us a desire for excellence, and nearly all Christians wrestle with feelings of having failed in some way. Some folks live with remorse that plagues them for years.

What can we do about this? We can receive the incredible forgiveness that Jesus came to give us.

Peter made a horrible mistake when he denied that he ever knew Jesus. If in his despair, he had committed suicide, he would never have known the joy that soon came to him. Think of the excitement he must have felt when: *People brought the sick into the streets and laid them on beds and mats so that at least Peter's shadow might fall on some of them as he passed by. Crowds gathered also from the towns around Jerusalem, bringing their sick and those tormented by evil spirits, and all of them were healed* (Ac. 5:15-16).

God has promised each of us His forgiveness for all our failures. Have you made mistakes that have been pulling you downward? Now is the perfect time to be set free, because Jesus gives you the gift of His righteousness. Like Paul, we can *be found in him, not having a righteousness of my own that comes from the law, but that which is through faith in Christ* (Ph. 3:9).

None of us deserve this forgiveness and righteousness. We can do nothing to erase our past failures, but we can all be forgiven and made whole by our faith in Jesus.

Often we accept His forgiveness for our past failures, but when we make one TODAY, we feel miserable. The joy of receiving forgiveness is so great that Paul wrote in Ro. 5:20: *Where sin increased, grace increased all the more*.

The more mistakes we make, the more grace we receive! To be sure we would not misunderstand this principle, Paul says in verse 22: *What shall we say, then? Shall we go on sinning so that grace may increase? By no means!* And also in verse 15: *Shall we sin because we are not under law but under grace? By no means!*

This is the miracle: The more we receive God's forgiveness, the stronger our zeal to obey Him becomes!

When we realize that we have made a mistake, we must repent and receive God's forgiveness as quickly as possible. Then our joy keeps increasing.

A Happy Stomach

When our stomachs are full, the house is warm and our health good, we can be lulled into a false sense of peace. Why change if everything is fine?

But an empty stomach gets our attention. It wants to be fed. An empty bank account demands action. A hurting body cries out for help. All these afflictions compel us to *do something*. And they often move us to seek God's help.

Our hearts may be starving for the joy that only God can give. If we are unhappy and complain because our circumstances have not changed, we are blaming God. To blame God may *seem* to be the easiest solution, but it is the best way to end up in trouble.

Society won't accept our excuses when we feel justified in breaking the law. Neither will God accept our excuses when we feel justified in grumbling about our problems. Notice His response when the Israelites complained: *The people complained about their hardships in the hearing of the LORD, and when he heard them his anger was aroused. Then fire from the LORD burned among them and consumed some of the outskirts of the camp* (Nu. 11:1).

Of course, the Jews believed their complaints were justified. Well, don't we all? I was once a "card-carrying" member of "grumblers incorporated." I complained at every inconvenience. I wanted my stomach to be full, to have plenty of money, and to have no problems. Even as a Christian I grumbled many times every day. I am grateful that not only did God hear me, He also corrected me. He helped me to see that complaining is exactly the opposite way to get Him to do anything to help us.

Paul understood this. In Philippians 2:14, he wrote: *Do everything without complaining or arguing.* I argued with God as I begged Him to change my "terrible circumstances." But *He did nothing*. Then I learned the secret of how to get my needs met. I began to thank Him for things *just as they were.* I fell back into

178

my old habit of complaining many times, but each time I repented, and asked Him to help me do better. As I learned to obey God's command to *Give thanks always for all things,* I became increasingly happy. He *then* began to shower me with blessings that were above anything I could ever have asked for.

Do you understand now, why I am so enthusiastic about trying to convince everyone to praise God? The solution to everyone's problems is exactly the same: We *must* stop complaining about the negative things that God permits in our lives, and concentrate instead on praising Him for *all* things. We should tell Him over and over again that we trust Him. When we do this, His joy will eventually control every part of our lives.

He Changes Our Tongues!

When I became a Christian I soon realized that I had much to learn regarding the way I used my tongue. For example, I read: *How you must rid yourselves of all such things as these: anger, rage...* (Col. 3:8).

At age fourteen I was already quite adept at cutting people down by the way I spoke to them. This was somewhat strange, since by nature I was a quiet, soft-spoken boy. In school, other students asked questions or raised their hands to answer questions, but I seldom spoke. When I became angry, however, bitter words sprang forth as if released by a tightly coiled spring.

As a new Christian I read the Bible for the first time, and often spent an entire day devouring it. The more I read, the more I knew I needed God's help to defeat the anger that still churned within me.

When I went into the Army at nineteen, my faith in God abated, and soon I fell back into my earlier anger. I seldom said much, but when I became angry my tongue would unleash a torrent of wrath. I recall confronting men who were much bigger and stronger than I, and threatening them with all sorts of violence. They must have sensed my intense anger for they always backed down.

When the Lord called me to preach, I thought He had made a big mistake. I felt that I didn't have anything to say. I had always preferred to keep quiet, and let someone else do the talking. But when my first opportunities came to preach, something happened. If they gave me an hour to speak, I didn't pause until the hour was finished. If I spoke to five, ten, or one hundred people, I never had the slightest trace of being nervous. I could stand up without any preparation and speak for any length of time. Sometimes I would preach for an entire hour and not even remember what I had said.

When an evil spirit was controlling my life, I spoke with rage. When I began to follow Christ, the Holy Spirit began to guide my tongue.

I've said all of this to emphasize that we can learn to let the Holy Spirit influence the way we talk. When He does, He can cause our words to help rather that hurt others.

People respond positively to a smile on our faces, and to the pleasant words that come from our lips. Have you ever noticed how you respond to a waitress? One waitress may serve you, and a few minutes later you can't remember which one she was. She made no impression on you. But if another waitress approaches you with a bright smile and greets you with cheery words, you pay attention to her. And you'll be inclined to reward her more generously at tip time!

God created us in such a way that we respond in kind to the emotions of others. If we permit the Holy

Spirit to control what comes from us, we can be used by God to help the hurting people around us. Then we are not limited to our natural, normal way of responding to people. The Spirit of God wants to change us so that we become better witnesses of what Christ has done for us.

I pray that the joy of Christ will bubble up within your heart in some new and powerful way. My life is proof that if we ask Him, Christ will give us hearts of joy and praise.

We Have the Keys

In Matthew 16:19 Jesus gives us an amazing promise: *I give you the keys of the kingdom*. With that promise in hand, we can unlock secrets.

The potential for hydrogen power has always been a reality, but until recent years it was one of nature's closely guarded secrets. But with today's knowledge and understanding, men can release that incredible power. Christ has supplied us the necessary "knowledge and understanding" for us to release the incredible power of His joy. His joy releases His happiness in us! With that understanding we can achieve the peace of heart that is described in Philippians 4:7 (TLB): *You will experience God's peace, which is far more wonderful than the human mind can understand*.

Just as God's peace is *far more wonderful than the human mind can understand*, His joy can lift us above the circumstances of our lives. In fact, this joy is often *increased* when surrounded by the most difficult of circumstances. It's a little like an explosive.

As a Demolition Expert in World War II, I learned to surround a small amount of explosive with steel, or other hard material. When the explosive was ignited, the pressure created by the material around it would magnify its explosive power.

Just as the steel initially confines the explosive material, you may be surrounded by difficulties that *seem* to confine you in a prison of unhappiness, and to prevent joy from ever being released in you. But those same difficulties may be the very material that God wants to use to cause His power to do wonderful things in your life! Jesus was nailed to a cross, sealed in a tomb and seemingly defeated. But then God caused His life-giving power to propel Jesus from death to life.

You may not personally know anyone who knows how to release hydrogen power, but you still believe that hydrogen power can be released. You may not personally know anyone who understands the power of God's joy, but please believe it is real! Jesus said His keys are available. Notice that He said "keys," in the plural. As you learn to use them, please share them with others. The more you give to others, the greater your own joy and happiness will become.

Postlude

Mary and I have read every page in this book many times. Each reading has increased our own joy. We encourage you to re-read each page.

If this book has been a blessing to you, please let us know. Every month we prepare *Praise News* in which we share new things that we learn about praise. We will be pleased to send this to you at no charge, on request. You can contact us at:

Merlin Carothers/Foundation of Praise
PO Box 2518, Dept. B19
Escondido, CA 92033-2518
www.merlincarothers.com

About the Author

Merlin Carothers' books have been translated into 47 languages. A Master Parachutist in the 82nd Airborne Division, he served as a guard to General Dwight D. Eisenhower in World War II. Later, as a Lt. Colonel in the U.S. Army Chaplaincy he served in Europe, Korea, the Dominican Republic, Panama and Vietnam. He is a pilot, lecturer and retired pastor. He has made many television appearances and has traveled worldwide to share what he has learned about praising the Lord. Merlin and his wife Mary, live in San Marcos, California.

You will also want to read these other best-sellers by Merlin R. Carothers

PRISON TO PRAISE $3.95
Many people list this as the most unusual book they have ever read.Millions say it changed their lives and introduced them to the solution to their problems. This is not a book about a prison with bars, but about a prison of circumstances--and how to be set free!
PRISON TO PRAISE, VIDEO $12.95
POWER IN PRAISE $6.95
Three Million National Bestseller. A simple, clear explanation of how and why the principles introduced in *Prison to Praise* work in every day life.
ANSWERS TO PRAISE $6.95
Overjoyed Christians felt compelled to share with Merlin the "signs and wonders" they experienced while practicing the teachings of praise.

PRAISE WORKS! $6.95
More letters from an assortment of thousands illustrate the secret of *freedom through praise*.

WALKING AND LEAPING $6.95
When Merlin and his family rolled over a hill in their new car and trailer they praised the Lord and miracles happened!

BRINGING HEAVEN INTO HELL $6.95
Merlin shares new discoveries of how the Holy Spirit sheds light from heaven in the midst of a personal hell.

VICTORY ON PRAISE MOUNTAIN $6.95
Spontaneous praise often leads into valleys that are direct paths to higher ground.

THE BIBLE ON PRAISE $3.25
A beautiful four-color booklet featuring Merlin's favorite selected verses on praise from thirty-eight books of the Bible.

MORE POWER TO YOU $6.95
Written for persons in every day places who need more power in their every day lives.

WHAT'S ON YOUR MIND? $6.95
Would you be ashamed for everyone you know to see your thoughts? If so, you urgently need to read and understand W*hat's On Your Mind?*.

LET ME ENTERTAIN YOU $6.95
After years of serving the Lord Merlin was eager to retire. He wanted to rest, relax and enjoy a quiet life, but God had other plans for him.

PRAISE CLASSICS $11.95
Prison to Praise and *Power in Praise* in a hardcover edition.

FROM FEAR TO FAITH $6.95
God wants to be intimately involved in your life and help you have victory over your problems?

PLEASE ENCLOSE $3.00 FOR SHIPPING ON ALL ORDERS.